The
Plea of Pan

(1901)

Henry W. Nevisnson

ISBN 0-7661-0572-5

Request our FREE CATALOG of over 1,000
Rare Esoteric Books
Unavailable Elsewhere

Freemasonry * Akashic * Alchemy * Alternative Health * Ancient Civilizations * Anthroposophy * Astral * Astrology * Astronomy * Aura * Bacon, Francis * Bible Study * Blavatsky * Boehme * Cabalah * Cartomancy * Chakras * Clairvoyance * Comparative Religions * Divination * Druids * Eastern Thought * Egyptology * Esoterism * Essenes * Etheric * Extrasensory Perception * Gnosis * Gnosticism * Golden Dawn * Great White Brotherhood * Hermetics * Kabalah * Karma * Knights Templar * Kundalini * Magic * Meditation * Mediumship * Mesmerism * Metaphysics * Mithraism * Mystery Schools * Mysticism * Mythology * Numerology * Occultism * Palmistry * Pantheism * Paracelsus * Parapsychology * Philosophy * Plotinus * Prosperity & Success * Psychokinesis * Psychology * Pyramids * Qabalah * Reincarnation * Rosicrucian * Sacred Geometry * Secret Rituals * Secret Societies * Spiritism * Symbolism * Tarot * Telepathy * Theosophy * Transcendentalism * Upanishads * Vedanta * Wisdom * Yoga * *Plus Much More!*

KESSINGER PUBLISHING, LLC

http://www.kessingerpub.com

email: books@kessingerpub.com

THE PLEA OF PAN

BY THE SAME AUTHOR

NEIGHBOURS OF OURS: STORIES OF SHADWELL.

IN THE VALLEY OF TOPHET: STORIES OF THE BLACK COUNTRY.

THE THIRTY DAYS' WAR: SCENES IN THE WAR BETWEEN GREECE AND TURKEY.

LADYSMITH: THE DIARY OF A SIEGE.

CLASSIC GREEK LANDSCAPE AND ARCHITECTURE: NOTES TO JOHN FULLEYLOVE'S PICTURES IN GREECE.

DEDICATED TO

THE EARTH-MOTHER

To Earth, who bore the dragon broods,
Spawning beside the unnavigated waves
Devouring lizards with bats' wings;
Who housed a terror deep in woods,
And down the gulf of fiery caves
Wrought mammoths and plate-armoured things;

Who glories in the tiger's might,
And feeds the snake, sin's counterpart;
Who drinks the blood of clanging wars,
And bears through the silences of night
The melody of a lover's heart
Among the unchanged, untrodden stars.

CONTENTS

	PAGE
INTRODUCTION	ix
A NEW PHEIDIPPIDES	1
A PRIESTESS TO APOLLO	43
THE FIRE OF PROMETHEUS	85
VERTICORDIA	129

NOTE

Two of these Essays have appeared in the *Contemporary Review,* and are republished here by the Editor's kind permission

INTRODUCTION

ON THE SAVAGE SOUL

It may seem as though there were hardly room in the modern world for the few simple savages that still exist. They are survivals from an age not far remote in time, but irretrievable as the dinornis. Amid the drab security of civilisation they wander like captive Indians on parole. Present creeds and ideals do not greatly concern them. They have never been wholly dipt in urbanity, but are like the Celts of early days when British Christianity was at odds with heathendom, and high-hearted mothers left the right arms of their babies unchristened, so that they might strike the stronger blow. They long for the sun, the moon, the stars, and the desert air. In the midst of daily life, in sober streets where policemen rot at ease, in committee-rooms and on boards of education, in quiet rectories and legislative assemblies, a breath of the wilderness comes suddenly, and whispers in their ears. At once the dull horror of all this sedentary world is borne in upon them.—The old spirit wakes and cries for the wings of the morning that it may fly away and bid sewage and civilisation go hang.

Some strive, and not in vain, to still the cry of that wild desire with sports and literature. They gallop after foxes, or spend a fortune to kill one stag. The poorer of them shoot pigeons from traps, or give the rat five leaps for his life on Wormwood Scrubbs. Some souse themselves in tales of rapiers and the heather oozing red; or by the cushioned fireside they haunt the incense-laden ages, when the pennon fluttered from the castle wall, and cheery decorators were occupied with

INTRODUCTION xi

handicrafts in the cheaping-stead below. Some go back to fairyland, and drive the brazen cars with Fergus, or with Niam of the golden hair cross the ocean to reach that unchanging land:

> 'Which lies far off in the golden west,
> On the verge of a golden sea.'

Happy are they. But for those who lack this enviable gift of illusion—for those whose imagination is not strong enough to encase them as in an enchanted and many-coloured shrine, holding them uncontaminated and undistressed amid the common dulness or glare of to-day—what remains for them? They are not poetic enough to be put off with cultivated stags within reach of comfortable shooting-boxes. To them the largest caged rat never appears like a lion in the wild, nor are the ruins of the past to be revived by lingering with tender regret over their stones and bones. It is true they love the romantic visions of old days quite as much as the poets can. How gladly would they have sailed with Drake, searching the Spaniard among dim-discovered islands. They love the jewelled twilight of knightly quests and demon rocks and the lonely chapel bell. To them it would not seem strange to worship at Stonehenge, to hunt and fight through life among forms vanishing in the forest and voices calling from stormy headlands amid the rain. It is as though they had themselves come from a country full of such scenes, and a regretful spirit were always crying to them to return. But perhaps it is that their life is not sufficiently spiritual to wrap them round in an atmosphere of an affectionately imagined past, such as poets and theologians breathe. Draw down the blinds of make-believe as they may, they cannot shut out the reality of this present and civilised world. And so they remain uncomforted and distraught —clipped cranes beside an ornamental water, huntsmen in an exhibition, worshippers who have outlived their god.

At times in Ireland a red wind sweeps up from the sea. It bears the sorrowful dust of all the exiles whose bones first grew under the heart of that sad land. In death they are returning from their innumerable banishments, that their dust may rest again upon her lap. To them that sorrowful peace is not forbidden. But us the red wind might bear in vain round the earth's girdle, following the sun. That wild star which was our mother, is vanishing from under heaven. She is harried and burnt; her streams are fouled, her forests cut down. Her wild beasts are slaughtered for pleasure, her heroic cities converted into communities of mice. She has lost the incalculable variety, the careless incertitude which made the life of her sons so dangerous and so sweet. From birth to death each man and woman seems to twist one tiny thread as in a clanking loom, and, compared to our rugged ancestry, the indistinguishable and misshapen swarms of to-day would appear unendurably unhappy, did they but know their wretchedness. But a few know it, and like the girl in the old Connaught song they may cry: 'A thousand farewells to last night! It is my grief that it was not to-night which came first.'

Too long have we been in exile. Increase of wealth, mechanical inventions, clubs, upholstery, waterworks, schools, medicine, madhouses, reformatories, orphan-asylums, law-courts, prisons, and all the other varieties of moral soap—how irrelevant they seem to the simple savage! The desperate widow in *Democracy* doubted if it were worth while to make two blades of grass grow where one grew before, and certainly to set two bulging, flap-footed gentlemen to stand on a flagstone instead of one, seems an unworthy aim for evolution after all its labours. The more the worse, says the savage when he sees them; the more the worse, he says as he watches the lines of ignoble streets blotting out the fields with hutches for the suburban species; the more the worse, as he hears the mill-hands scurrying to the factory while the hooter screams. Forlorn in exile, he takes his staff and goes to find some scattered traces of his country. He seeks her under the long night of the poles, or in the ancient valleys of Asia, or beside rivers where old behemoth still lurks in the covert of the reed. He often sees her mirage just in front. Sometimes he imagines he has crossed the borders into her wilds, and for a moment he is full of joy. But he finds that the land knows him no more. Her life is no longer his. She seems to ask why he is changed. Or she regards him with polite and slightly contemptuous suspicion. In the midst of the few poor ruins of his home, he stands as a spectator, a tourist, an extraneous patron, a curious investigator, a Saturday-to-Monday guest. He is in danger of writing a book.

It remains for him to inhabit the 'Redskins' Reserve,' the 'Indian Territory' of the soul; not a bad substitute, for it is very large and his freehold for existence. Without for a moment quitting the reality of modern life, he lives within that spiritual territory, untrammelled, unlegalised, and unstaled in thought or deed. There he may hunt for all that is quick with life, and there may find the quality of the wild and ancient earth, so spontaneous, prodigal, and unconscious of offence. On the other side of custom's thick-set hedge, we may still see the eyes of wild spirits gleaming, and if we watch in silence they will draw near. It is only in the air of golden mediocrity that they cannot breathe, for they are keen and finely tempered as a blue sword. With them the savage soul has his dwelling, lying in wait for any point where extremity is reached. He lives by danger, hardship, and uncalculating extravagance of self. He may live in serried orchestras, in Dantean devotion, and Hannibalic invasions; but no less he lives among the scattered lumps that strew a battlefield, or the unknown women lamenting them at home; and he may be inspired by the three successive notes of a pierced reed.

Only within the limits of this Indian Territory can the savage soul maintain the savage and first-hand excellence which acts from its own unconscious and inexorable nature. Only here he really exists, and for love of this land, his native country, he is always searching for those moments of existence when danger is most dangerous, and difficulty most severe. With sinews steeled as a cowboy's, he will go questing through life, rejoicing in the contest's peril, and encouraged by the discovery of any comrade who will share his warfare. For he will never cease from war, and it was not without reason that the poet sang of the Happy Warrior, and not of the Happy Bagman, the Happy Landlord, the Happy Member of Parliament, or the Happy Priest. Against the mediocre, the average, the good-enough, the savage soul wages war without quarter, and disdains, as Montaigne said, in the catalogue of his true duties, all easy, faint, ordinary, and provincial rules.

Having entered upon this unsurveyed territory, in which every step is as truly a discovery as the exploration of Erebus, he may pass through the outer world with a wandering but friendly heart, assured of comradeship, not only in wharfs and coal-pits, but even in respectable houses. If it be his happy fortune to haunt the earthly sea, wild mountains, and such desert as remains, his knowledge of that still wilder land will cause him to hear finer voices on the wind, and to see more brilliant hues within the rainbow.

In the commonest hovel of the bog he may discover that extreme and untamed spirit which is akin to goats and gods. He is shy, that blended soul of earth and ether. He loves to hide by moorland streams, to labour in folded valleys, or hang from cliffs that face the sunset. Yet at times we may catch sight of him in drawing-rooms or lurking under a judge's throne, and then we rejoice to find him still alive and quite on speaking terms with all who are a little like himself.

I

A NEW PHEIDIPPIDES

It happened once that I was in Greece at a time when the country was not so familiar to us as it became during the Turkish invasion. In spite of its beauty and associations, it was not a very attractive place to the average Englishman. There was good bathing in the Ægæan, and pretty fair climbing on Olympus, but no fishing to speak of, and hardly any sport at all. The Duke of Sparta had some moderate shooting in Elis. There was talk of boars and wolves upon Cithæron still, but I could not get a sight of any. The brigands were very nearly exterminated, and in fact I saw no game, beyond a few hares at Sunium, and some snipe on the Alpheus. Plenty of eagles, of course; and at Mycenæ I watched a Greek native practising at one with an old muzzle-loader; but the real local sport is to fire pistols into old temple columns at twelve paces. For there are any number of ruins and things about, though to the ordinary Englishman they are rather like our grandmothers' love-scenes — pretty in their day, but no special concern of ours.

And yet, as I dawdled through the country on one pony or another, I saw a few queer things, and perhaps the queerest of all was a god. Of course there was nothing remarkable in the mere fact of encountering such a being; many people have seen a god before now, and there was no reason why I should not see one, too, if he happened to be about. But the peculiarity of the event lay in the god's personality. He was not much to look at, poor old boy, but a rare fellow to talk, and he said some unusual things, which I cannot remember completely; for indeed he was not talking actually to me, but to a fellow named Gordon, whom I had met the evening before at a little town high up in the mountains in Arcadia. I took him for a don at first, because he was so detestably polite, and kept calling my pony a mule, and knew his way about Greece without a 'Baedeker.' We slept in one room on a fairly clean rug, and he woke me at half-past four, and from the window I saw Erymanthus, a long range of square-topped mountains, just beginning to look grey with their snows against the sky of night. In Greece they save you a lot of time by not giving you anything to wash in. So, before five we were out in the dirty street with two little ponies and a guide. We were going to see a famous old temple, and the country round was certainly very beautiful. The stony track went straight into the hills directly we left the little town, and we crossed two high passes, and made our way through uninhabited valleys, and round the heads of water-courses, and through woods of a bushy kind of fir, and over stretches of green, covered with all manner of flowers and shrubs, where some early nightingales were trying to get their notes in tune, and hoopoes went flitting about like woodpeckers pretending to be butterflies. After some three hours' climbing we came to the top of the highest spur from the central range, and there, just in front of us, two or three hundred yards down, we saw the grey columns of the temple itself. Nearly all are still standing, and I think nearly every one would have thought them rather fine, all alone out there in the hills. We lay down on a lot of thyme and other plants close outside the temple, having a view of the sea in two places, on each side the Messenian promontory; and, far away in the south, the mountains of Taygetus, down by Sparta, ran up into sharp peaks like the Alps, covered with snow. The guide sat behind us with the ponies, and began playing with his string of beads—the only intellectual exercise of a modern Greek. Then I asked Gordon if he wouldn't tell me something about the temple.

'I know nothing particular about it,' he said; 'not half so much as "Baedeker."'

So I told him not to pretend to be a worse prig than heaven made him. And I thought I heard some one laugh behind us, but I could only see the Greek staring sleepily at his beads.

'Well,' said Gordon, 'the temple was built as a thankoffering to Apollo the Giver of Health, and was designed by the same architect as the temple of Apollo's sister at Athens. It stands on the site of an old shrine of Pan, who, of course, was worshipped in all this pastoral district.'

'Yes,' I said, 'but I want to know who Pan really was, and why one god could drive out the worship of another; and what the priests thought of their god, and how they served him, out on the mountains here.'

'I'm sorry,' said Gordon, 'but I know nothing about the priests, and next to nothing about Pan. Only, it doesn't seem strange that a half-brutish conception like him—the rude god of an innocent but distinctly provincial Arcadia—should be superseded by the worship of Apollo in his purest and kindliest form—the Destroyer turned to Healer, the scorching fire tempered and diffused into the genial light of such a morning as this. He is indeed the god of my idolatry. It is his priest that I would always be.'

'Bless my soul!' I said, looking round at him, and seeing that his eyes were fixed on the distance.

'Even now,' he went on, 'in such a

place as this, one may be conscious of a sense of healing, of purification, in the cool air and the freshness of the mountains. The current of life again runs clear, and the power of the eye is restored. The mind itself is pervaded with a purity as of sunrise. The human passions then appear to it gross and almost inconceivable, like the grotesque monsters of creation's early slime. It is not to be believed that they should dominate or allure a thing so fine and shapely as the spirit has then become. Envy, ambition, and desire then appear to us ridiculous, distorted, and in the truest sense obscene. Guided by an increasing discernment, the soul becomes rigorous in selection of her proper food, and rejects all that is unclean, or tainted with commonplace, or spoilt by superfluity. It is no drug which is thus given by the god; for the gift is health itself, and health needs no healing. To his service the soul willingly bows, that in it she may attain to freedom. Therefore she lays on herself the limits which are the doors into space, and girding herself with restraints, she hastens to the fruition of the brief but high rewards which open upon her rigorous course. At every step her delicacy of choice increases; her demand for purity and decorous beauty becomes more exacting. But at every step also her frame becomes more tightly strung, and her purpose more strenuous. Then in the heart is built up, stone by stone, a temple such as this, fit house for a male god, a home of grave liberty, such as springs from laws self-imposed and self-justified. That is the Apollo whose priest I would be, here on the site of his ancient shrine. You see how stern the country is for all its beauty, how manlike in contrast with the feminine rapture of such lands as Italy. I would have myself of a nature to match this land.'

'What's all that?' I said, for I was

getting rather sleepy, and only caught a few more sentences here and there.

'Our old master,' he went on, 'used to say, "Not what I have, but what I do, is my kingdom." But now we have taken one further step towards our redemption from vulgarity. — Not what we have, nor what we do, but what we are—that is our kingdom now. And what we are depends upon a long series of choice—those brief but eternal acts of choice—self-imposed limits which are the assurance of man's strength and of his ultimate spiritual emancipation.'

After that, his voice was mixed up with the bees and the calling of birds, and all the other quiet noises of a calm day, and they were united in my head into a kind of orchestra played by fairies, only that now and then I seemed to hear a low clear note of a flute coming nearer and nearer. And after a time I was slowly awakened by a vague feeling that we were not alone. So at last I looked round to where Gordon had been sitting, rather behind me on the right, and between me and him I saw the great hindquarters of some dark and shaggy beast.

'Talk about the Father of the Goats, indeed!' I thought, and, drawing my gun towards me without moving a leaf, I raised myself on my elbows till, inch by inch, I exposed his hairy side. The whole thing seemed queer, of course, but I was too excited to think, and was on the point of jumping up to bring him down as he ran clear, when I heard a deep, low voice, with a kind of laugh in it, speaking.

'I'm afraid, sir,' it said, 'you wouldn't approve of me, for it's hard to find any limit on my poor old body.'

Down went my gun. No doubt most sportsmen will think me a fool to lose a chance of bagging a god. I might have taken his skin home, done up in my rugs; and have hung his head in my ancestral hall, stuffed.

But I didn't fire. To shoot a beast that could talk seemed too much like firing on a mob. He was stretched on the ground deep in flowers, with his head propped between his hands. His face was like the bust of Socrates in our old headmaster's room at school; and there was the queerest look of amusement on it, mixed with a kind of melancholy too, as though he were a little tired with all he had seen. The Greek had disappeared. Gordon was talking as though nothing unusual had happened. For myself, I felt like Balaam.

'Even if you don't approve of me,' the god went on, 'it's a comfort to see you're not frightened.'

'We moderns,' said Gordon, 'are never frightened—only infinitely curious.'

'Infinite is a dangerous word, you know,' said the god. 'But my poor mother wasn't at all modern, for when I was born, she ran away at sight of me, and my supposed father had to get a rabbit's skin to wrap his furry baby in, and carry me up to the gods, who at once began that sad habit of making puns on my name. But that has always been the way with me; a terror one moment, a joke the next, I am like the People's Vote.'

'Your presence was better than a vote in battle,' said Gordon.

'Ah, sir,' said the god, with a modest sigh, 'that's a very long time ago.'

'Forgive my saying so,' said Gordon after a pause, 'but it's very strange to find you still alive. We have been told so very often of your death, both by fishermen and poets.'

'Yes,' said the god, smiling. 'I'm afraid it was a wicked story of mine— that voice of lamentation heard over the evening sea round Paxos. You see, it is better to give up certain things than wait till they give you up. At least, I've heard lovers say it is so with love. And may it not be the same with life?'

'He that loseth his life shall find it,' said Gordon.

'It is a true saying,' said the god. 'Think of poor old Zeus—a deity of some real importance in his day. But when his old way of life began to moulder, he clung to it with such brutal avidity that he was rotten long before he was buried, and is now only remembered by jokes on his domestic relations, as a kind of Henry VIII. whose first wife was unfortunately immortal.'

'Good Heavens!' said Gordon, 'what do you know of Henry VIII.?'

'Ah, sir,' said the god sadly, 'I see that, like the rest, you always forget I am still alive. Or do you suppose I have slept all these years, like the Seven of Ephesus?'

'I beg your pardon, I'm sure,' said Gordon, 'but you must own it's a little hard to connect you with modern life.'

'Hard for the citizens of your great towns, no doubt,' said the god. 'How should they find room for the sun-burnt god of the hymn in my praise, the god who loves soft rivers and deep woods:

> and at fall of night
> Returning, bids the valleys in their sleep
> Listen to strains surpassing all the might
> Of that sad bird who, tortured by the spring,
> Her yearning lamentation honey-sweet doth
>   sing?

Yes, in modern cities no doubt it is hard, but here in Arcadia surely you might suppose even my old pastoral form to survive.'

'It is very refreshing to find it so,' said Gordon; 'but this new railway round your own Mount Parthenion must be rather intrusive on your solitude.'

'Oh, I don't so much mind,' said the god, 'except that it kills my special breed of tortoises there. The train can't help going faster than they, and it overtakes them as they bask along the lines. Still, I like to revisit Arcady for a holiday now and then, and as it is holiday-

A NEW PHEIDIPPIDES

time, I'll go my way, bidding you a triple farewell.'

'Oh, please don't go,' said Gordon, laying his hand on the shaggy side.

'Nay,' said the god, 'you'll soon forget me. Even Athens forgot me, you know. You clever people always do.'

'But if one could be your second Pheidippides?' said Gordon.

'No, really I'd rather go,' answered the god. 'I'm afraid I'm hardly modern enough to talk about nothing but myself with grace. I've always been behind the times.'

'At least,' said Gordon, 'tell me where you are to be found again.'

'I go to and fro upon the earth,' said the god, 'like him who has long caused my form and attributes to be blasphemed. And I have many outward semblances, and yet but one true form. The Egyptians knew it, though, as the historian says, they figured me under this pastoral shape as a matter of pious convenience. Also they knew that I was of the elder gods, compared to whom this Apollo here and his blue-stockinged sister are but upstarts of yesterday, separated from that early creation by clean-cut limits such as seem so greatly to delight you.'

'It was mental limit of which I spoke,' said Gordon—'a certain definiteness of mood and vision.'

'Mental limit, no doubt,' said the god; 'but may not such limit be signified in the outward form? These purified gods of yours were cut off from our old creation, and bore no remembrance of the pleasant furry animals upon their marble limbs. Eyes peered at them shyly from the thickets, wondering what those white and naked shapes might be. Before they came, we were a merry crew together, Centaurs and Sphinxes and Titans, Gorgons and Hydras and Chimæras dire— a wanton pack of cross-bred cousins. It was then often hard to tell where the beast left off and the god began: as hard as it still is on my poor body, if I guess your thought aright. In those days lions and wolves held equal converse with gods, and in men's ears the birds sang the words as well as the music of all their pretty tales of love and fairy travel. Then came the change, which I myself should not have escaped, had I not hidden myself away with the shepherds here, hedged in by barriers of mountains from that cold and inhuman thing, the sea, which is always on the side of change.

'When at last I ventured to emerge, stealing down the river-beds at night into rich Elis, or along the broad hollow of Lacedæmon, all was over. The comrades of earth's prime were gone, and I was left like an orphan of another race. The new gods did not even pay me the compliment of fear, but in educated scorn they laughed at my homely appearance.

I let them have it their own way, perceiving that the fashion of laughter is the most fleeting of things. And for service I attached myself to the Great Mother, a solemn goddess, whom I chose because, when first she looked on me, I perceived kindly rain and sunshine mingled in her face. Her I served so faithfully that some Olympian wit called me the Mother's dog-of-all-work, and I proudly bore the name. In her praise I sang with bands of mountain girls in front of the Theban poet's door all night long. Those summer nights of music, when Cithæron looked dreamy and lower than his height under the moon, are far behind me now. The Mother is almost forgotten. The poet's words are scarcely understood, and Thebes is for the tenth time in ruins. Yet I am here, still living on, though rather fallen from my estate, which I admit was never high.'

The god laughed cheerfully, and Gordon said: 'I do not wish to seem at all impolite, but it is certainly a little strange that you, of all others, should be the only survivor.'

'I don't wonder at your surprise,' said the god. 'The worshippers of Apollo are able to rise to an airy height which I can hardly conceive; and, like the man who went up to heaven on a beetle, they think that we poor children of earth look very small from that distance. Nevertheless, it almost seems as if there must be some everlasting quality about my worshippers and me. For I am certainly alive, and a god lives only so long as he has worshippers.'

'And who are his worshippers?' asked Gordon.

'Those who are like him,' said the god.

'But what, then, is the everlasting quality of which you spoke?'

The god sat silent for a time, with the puzzled look of a ploughboy when the parson inquires after his spiritual condition.

'Can you imagine,' he answered at

length, 'a quality which is common to wild animals and children and the poor?—shall we add women, too? perhaps it were wiser not.'

'I can indeed dimly apprehend some such quality,' said Gordon, 'but I could give it no name.'

'Neither can I give it a name,' said the god, 'any more than you can give a name to your own soul. I can but repeat what once the Great Mother told me. There are, she said, certain classes of beings which seem to stand at the meeting-place of many far-reaching and divergent powers. They appear to be haunted by dim associations, unconscious relationships. The fibres of their roots seem still to spring from the womb of earth, and with her breasts they are fed. But on another side they are no less full of promises of something beyond the rest of nature, as though they were always reaching out towards mysterious powers which may never be realised.

As a reasonable fact we know there are certain things they will not and cannot do. But if they did them, it would be absurd to feel much surprise. Those two ponies on which you and your friend rode up from the village—how full of zeal and rivalry the younger of them was! trembling with energy, maddened by reproof, exalted by praise, dashing hot-blooded into every difficulty, and struggling through it with tempestuous impatience. How small was the difference between him and a boy warrior, the glory of his men, whom his passionate mistakes so often lead into death! And the old mare, so wise and humble, trustworthy at every step—was she not a nurse of ninety years? That shepherd, too, whom you met on the way; night and day he lives with his flock; did he not seem to be one with the winds and hills? It would not have seemed strange if his sheep had said, Good morning, and he had bleated.'

'It is an old conceit of satirists,' said Gordon, 'that many men would more fully express their emotions by neighing, or howling, or braying.'

'Ah, yes, those satirists!' said the god; 'they were always much too clever for humble people like me. But let me rather tell you of a sight I once saw when the Great Mother suffered me to look into the inmost recess of her strange old workshop. She was standing, with a large apron on, before a kind of kneading-trough, and was fashioning mortal things. On one side of her, quicker than thought, flew a current of a brilliant blue element, hardly denser than air. On the other moved a sluggish and heavy stream of dark-red mud. And from it issued the fragrance of a fresh-ploughed field after rain. Into these two streams the Mother kept dipping a hand on each side, and clutching up random quantities; but the greater part of both went by unused, and what became of it I could not see.

After each dip the Mother brought her hands sharply together, and the two substances rushed into each other with a cry of joy, and became joined—oh, more closely than ever lovers were! She then began to mould them into shape in her trough. But they, in their passionate desire for living, continually thwarted her skill, so that in despair she often let them have it their own way. For she was in much haste, grudging every wave of the streams that passed unused. I saw her making a second Achilles, but his struggles to begin life so delayed her that she just finished him off as a wolf-hound, keen of eye and swift of foot. Another Cleopatra, too, was almost moulded, when she writhed away without her legs and arms, and lived alone in an island jungle as a magical white snake. The legs and arms were used for another woman, who drove men mad, and nobody knew why. And sometimes, after the Mother had begun upon an animal, the humour would take her to convert it into a man, whence come those people whom we naturally call bearish, or swinish, or apish, or proud as peacocks. But as for those whom, according to her intent, she succeeded in making into men in spite of their wrigglings, I observed that at times she appeared especially pleased with her results, like a dyer when he has hit just the right proportions for his dye. For then the two substances in their passionate union were converted into a kind of warm-blooded marble, and out of that she made the most excellent sorts of man.'

'Such as the poets, I suppose?' said Gordon.

'One or two of them, perhaps, were poets,' answered the god: 'but there were others, nor were they uncommon, though often they slipt away unnoticed into some unexplored recess of time. Whether or not they did anything memorable appeared to be merely a matter of circumstance; for all that they did sprang from the very composition of their nature, so that their greatest achievements were in fact no less natural than their eating and drinking. About them hung a sense of security and assurance, as of a sunshiny day, and they acted not in compliance with maxims but under an impulse derived from the wholesome admixture of their own being, like the divine instinct which guides a dog or pigeon home without the aid of finger-posts or governmental charts.'

'If all were like that,' said Gordon, 'we should be a community of saints indeed!'

'Oh, don't be too sure!' said the god, smiling. 'One or two saints were certainly of this kind, but all were not saints. Only, whether their deeds were good or evil, there was something inevitable and simple about them, as about the powers of nature, whether destructive or benign. However, it was not of them I wished to speak, but of two other kinds in whom I perceived every degree and variety of being, except that all fell short of that ultimate grace. For it would often happen that, when the Mother clutched a handful of the flowing mud, some would ooze through her fingers and be lost. Then she would sigh over the resulting forms, though they were of a strange and fantastic beauty, and seemed even to shine with a delicate light of their own, like sea-things two or three days dead. Indeed, I was quite overcome by their elegance and charm, for they tripped away into the world with an airy step, and every moment I expected to see them take flight and hover down the path like butterflies. So in my wonder I asked the Mother why she sighed over them. But she was trying to squeeze some heavy lumps of mud into shape, and answered: " I can hardly tell you now, for I'm busy knocking a little decency into these silly monsters. But if you look at those pretty creatures a little closer you will find they are like bricks made without straw, having little constancy and endurance. And though they are now as gay as gossamers, and congratulate themselves aloud on their superiority to these other queer beings of mine, their fate is not really enviable."

'So I watched a while, and found that her words came true. For on reaching the harsh atmosphere of the upper world these delicate figures appeared like people who have ventured abroad in the cold too thinly clad. They shivered at every breath, and smarted even when nothing touched them. The common sights and sounds of earth appeared to them all too rude and crude. Over some, indeed, poverty extended a covering of its own, and the encrusting mire of daily necessity served as skin and cloak. But the most were able to avoid poverty, and if common dirt touched them they carefully scraped it off, leaving their flesh quivering and sore. And some were so deluded as confidently to maintain their own super-excellence, and to publish guides whereby others might strive to approach it. Like the fox which had lost its tail, they proclaimed it the duty of everybody to become like themselves, and they dared to pity those who had not reached that state. Therefore they called themselves friends of man, but took care to retain a scrupulous distance between themselves and the objects of their friendship. Others, standing more decidedly aloof, choked up the vulgar channels of sense by delicious artifices, like the crew of Ulysses, though it was not Sirens that they feared. They devoted themselves mainly to the practice of a quality called Intellectuality, about which people like me may hardly venture to speak. Indeed, their solemnity much impressed me, and, like the initiated, they seemed to possess some inner secret which gave a value to their words and ways; for it is impious to suppose them created in vain.

'But in the end, even in their case, I learnt the reason of the Mother's sighs, seeing that, for want of due admixture with the earthy loam, the glimmering blue substance itself began to grow thin and pale, being lost in air, or fading like a dyed cloth too often washed. The best and unhappiest among them, conscious of the native beauty of their souls, but shrinking from this boisterous world, turned to contemplation of themselves and criticism of their own growth or decay. Thus the soul was diverted to devour its own substance with a kind of lustful appetite, amidst unimaginable suffering, and the day of death alone put an end to the torment. So self-centred and subtle did they become that in face of choice they could hesitate for ever.

Many a one have I seen, at the meeting of two suburban roads, bewailing his lot and crying: "Here I stand. I can do either. The devil damn me!" No poison of Colchis or Median torture was ever so cruel as the suffering of such hesitation, and the sharpness of the pain did not deaden the gnawings of a vanity unappeased as the eagle of Prometheus. Nevertheless, unlike the cheery crowd which flings away life for a straw, the victims clung to it with pitiless anxiety, shuddering at hardship or danger. And so, with pain and disgust they trod their own blood in the wine-press, and prayed that their torment might never cease.'

'It is surely,' said Gordon, 'some circle of hell you describe, and not a race of the living.'

'I describe what I saw,' answered the god; 'and yet it is perhaps hard for me to be kindly towards them; for between them and my worshippers there is war without herald.'

'Again I ask you,' said Gordon, 'who these worshippers of yours may be?'

The god smiled to himself, and gently rubbed his shaggy legs together.

'Ah,' he said, 'I have told you that my worshippers are like myself; but indeed I do not know whether I ought not rather to call myself the worshipper of them. In love, you know, it is hard to say which is the lover and which the beloved. And so it is with the gods and their worshippers. And, as a lover pines when his mistress is far away, or is debarred from him by some separable spite, so that he can hardly be said to live till he can again touch the hem of her garment, so should I pine and wither without those quaint lovers of mine; and if they were to cease altogether, I should necessarily die. But it is impious to have such fears, though to some people my fears are hopes.'

'What fears or what hopes?' asked Gordon.

'Let us go back,' said the god, 'to the Great Mother at her kneading-trough. You remember, we left her laughing over some lumps of mud, into which she was trying to knock a little decency. In their making it appeared that part of the blue etherial substance had streamed away like smoke, and vanished before the union was complete. Grotesque and ungainly creatures they were, moving heavily along, very close to the ground, from which, in fact, they seldom dared to look up for fear of missing their sustenance. Mingled with them swarmed the insects and water-things and birds, and wild beasts innumerable. All had a share in the etherial substance, but in some, as in slugs and shellfish, it was almost hidden, whereas in the others it burnt and shone with a kind of longing, like a prisoner behind bars. And whenever I saw that look, whether in the eye of rat or bird or lion, a strange affection possessed me, as though the creatures were parts of myself, and had been separated from me recently and by accident. And I could have taken them to my heart, as a girl takes her baby, only that I feared the laughter of the superior gods. But the Great Mother smiled, and said: "My dear Pan, if you would do me a service, continue to watch over these wild things. You see how sweet and excellently fashioned they are. Nevertheless, this will not be your greatest task."

'And so, as the poets say, it is I who hear the shrill cries of the eagles robbed of their brood. I help the goat in her labour, and teach her to lick the kid all over with her blue tongue. I lurk in the forest when the tigers are full of love. I am in the look of the dog whom his master kicks. I count all the sorrows of the over-driven horse.'

'One would suppose,' said Gordon, 'that this charge alone gave you plenty to do.'

'Yes,' said the god; 'but you forget that I am both a god and a dog-of-all-work. This charge is but a small part of my labours. For, as I told you, I stand at the meeting of many ways, and each of them stretches to an invisible distance, like the high roads from Delphi, which is the navel of the earth. The same is true of my worshippers, who, as you remember, must necessarily be like me. It is as hard to find the limits on them as on my form, or to say which part is beast, which is man, and which is god. For into my especial care the Mother also delivered all those strange human figures which looked so brutish—nay, more brutish than the brutes. All of them are my working charge, and the poets were right in not limiting my lovingkindness to the shepherds of these hills alone. I sit beside the fisher all night, far out at sea in his lonely boat. He is rough and heavy, twisted with wet and cold; he smells of nets and fishes' scales; to me he is more beautiful than the great marble Poseidon of Melos. I stand with the hunter, waiting in the snow till the furry creatures pass. I know their swift pains and his joys, both. Grizzled, and dried like leather, in his old blue coat and bits of skins, he is fairer to me than naked Artemis. I am with the miner, hewing in his gallery under the earth; when the roof falls in, I hold his battered head. His mates say: "He wasn't a bad sort of man; now he must be buried." His wife and children cry, and I cry with them, more than for dead Zeus or an assassinated king. I hold the ploughshare with the ploughman, rejoicing in the damp earth and in the man who is so like it; no perfumed Dionysus smells so sweet. I teach queer tunes to the blind piper who raises a feeble whistle in your streets; trim Apollo, for all his lyre, never woke such music. I bathe with the boys in your brown river. The police carry off their scrappy shirts and trousers. They run naked over the slimy stones, more alert than Hermes, and more eloquent. I am with the soldier on the cool morning of battle, when he eats and drinks and curses, all for the last time. Beside him, Ares was a theatrical poser. I am with the tanned woman in the field, when she makes haste to feed her child, and cannot be quick enough, till suddenly it is still. Her eyes are softer than a cow's or Here's. But really you will think my worshippers a most disreputable and vulgar lot, quite incapable of understanding those joys of contemplation and the rigid selection of emotions by which you set so much store.'

'That's unfair,' said Gordon; 'none but the vulgar would accuse such people of vulgarity.'

'Nay, my son,' said the god, looking kindly on him, 'if I mock you, it is in self-defence. I care not, it is true, for the disdain with which your refined friends would regard me. With them I take delight in thrusting out my hoofs and displaying my goatish side. But alone, or among my worshippers, do you suppose I do not rejoice over our gleams of inexplicable reason, our consciousness of a yearning for we know not what, our moments of transforming passion, elevating us to the infinity of gods? Those translucent regions at which you aim may well have beauties and joys that we can hardly picture. I only ask to be remembered. It was the petition I sent to the old Athenians in their most pellucid air. Be not of those who from their sphere of white ideas cannot spare a glance into my world of sombre colours flecked with crimson. Is there no cause for marvel in that warm obscurity where I with my poor charges dwell amid the dust and slime of old earth? Like a torch-lit cave, it is illumined with half-lights shed from rare sparkles of the eternal fire. Is it no cause for worship that, unprotected in our gloom and squalor, from the midst of the daily efforts to stave off death by a little food and warmth, we who have been so long called ignoble, insensate, brutal, and depraved, should still for the most part find time for kindliness and laughter— for a sort of decency, if not beauty— and for a thing you might almost call virtue? O my son, keep your ear close against the ground, and you may still hear strange music. As in old days, when these Arcadians said I danced and sang in the valleys, you may still hear intermingled sounds of trampling and song echoing from all parts of the earth —the cries of birth and death, the rush of panic, and at times a sweet piping, ringing clear above the dirge of confused wailings and the alarms of drums. It is the wild and unpremeditated music of my children which you hear—the melody and recitative of old earth's opera, performed from age to age by an unconscious orchestra and choir, clustered around me at that meeting-place of profound and untraceable powers which lead far backward and far onward, repellent and opposite to all seeming, but ever striving to unite into a harmony of joy and sorrow.'

'Great is the power of opposites combined,' said Gordon. 'Love himself, we know, is the child of plenty and poverty.'

'Yes,' said the god; 'and you have but to look at my body to understand what a strange union of spiritual opposites went to its begetting. Nor must you think me in the least ashamed of it, red and brown and mingled as it is. The moon—the naked moon herself—one thin, white curve of loveliness—— O, you remember the tale:

"Arcadia, night, a cloud, Pan, and the moon!"

She scorned me not, she who scorned

others. Have I not reason to be proud?'

'Reason indeed,' said Gordon, 'to dream on that night through an immortal life.'

'And the Philosopher, too,' continued the god, 'do you suppose that he did not know what he was saying when he chose me of all the gods to whom to address his prayer for beauty in the inward soul? And he added, "May the outward and the inward man be at one?"'

'That was a prayer indeed!' said Gordon.

'And he would not have addressed it to me,' said the god, 'unless he had known that I possessed such unity of body and soul myself, and so could give it. So then, my dear fellow, when certain people make light of me and my worshippers, and call us low and brutish, I think upon the Moon and that Philosopher, and in those thoughts I find a consolation better than satire.

'But the sun just stands at noon, and you know what the poet says:

"Shepherd, 'tis not allowed when noon is high
To pipe as shepherds, for there's Pan to fear;
He, wearied with his hunting, turns to sleep,
And if we rouse him—O, the bitter rage!"

So, to maintain the poetic tradition, I must sleep now. It would never do to betray the poets, when they have said so many nice things about me. Therefore, farewell now, and, as the ghost says, remember me.'

He put a hand on Gordon's shoulder and was gone. Suddenly the air became still and heavy. The wind sighed, and sank. The sun himself seemed to halt and brood. The dogs barked no more in the valleys, and I did not hear the long, melancholy cry of the shepherds. Only a bee went on humming at a purple flower for a while, and then suddenly it ceased. I slept the sleep of the just even more sweetly than usual. When at last I woke, it must have been past two. The Greek was sitting beside the ponies again, playing with his beads. I looked for Gordon, but there was no trace of him, except that the grass where he had been was pressed down. When we got back to the little town, nobody had seen him, and I have never heard of him since.

For a moment I thought he was possibly Apollo himself, reduced to the position of a latter-day man of culture. But he wore trousers, and even Pan had not come to that. Though, to be sure, there is no saying what a god might not come to under a County Council.

II

A PRIESTESS TO APOLLO

'There was a city once as sick as ours;
Restless she lay upon her sea-washed throne,
Surmising evils.   For the gods were gone,
Their white homes shut ; no victim gay with flowers
Gladden'd her altars, but on all the towers
Vague terror sat, and women made their moan
From street to street, foreboding ; save alone
Where he who knew the mind of heavenly powers
Implored Apollo.
     But what Cretan old
Shall teach the lustral rite, and purify
Our country's slough, where pleasure coils with hate,
And hunger watches?   Who shall be so bold
As raise the healing prayer before she die?
And to what god shall she be dedicate?'

THESE lines by an unknown writer, referring, probably, to the purification of Athens by Epimenides, the Cretan, after the Cylonian crime, were lately recalled to my mind by a pleasant interview with which I was unexpectedly honoured. For on a clear day in early September

I was fortunate enough to meet again one of those ancient gods who, as is well known, still haunt this ancient world, and are recognised from time to time by the most unlikely people. The only strange thing about our meeting was its place. I was wandering upon mere English ground among Northumbrian moors, and instead of pursuing wisdom and the arts I was but poaching the habits of curlew and vipers, or whatever else I might pick up without unduly enraging the owners of earth. Making my way towards a line of hills which rose gradually from the wastes and fronted the north in sharp basalt cliffs, I crossed a long, straight road, green from disuse, and after wading through a bog of rushes and the Parnassus grass, began to climb the rising ground where a few mountain sheep with speckled faces and long yellow eyes were feeding among loose heaps of rock.

Suddenly I became aware that those

grey ruins of a mountain were not piled at random, but had been set in regular forms and angles, like the foundation walls of ancient buildings. And incredible old tales of history came into my mind, how that somewhere in this barbarous North, on the verge of Empire, severed from all the world, Rome had built a road and planted a wall, guarded at intervals by towns where dwelt the legions and generals far from the City. Could it be that those stony haunts of wheatears were relics left by the eagles? There stood the bases of the gates, round stone columns still rising two or three feet above the hawk-weed and brown partridge-grass. The pavement between them still showed the deep grooves worn by cart-wheels in days when horses understood the Roman tongue which cursed them as they bumped through the narrow entrance. I could trace the little streets, and the doors of the tiny houses, and the heating chambers for the baths, and the bakers' ovens. Near the middle lay the foundations of the Prefect's house, from which shivering senators had watched the sun go early down behind the grey bulwark of Cross Fell. And under the tufts of grass I tripped upon a stone which proved to be a short column still left lying on its side. Rolling it out of its trough in the reddish earth, where centipedes and innumerable ants and beetles scurried about like women in a revolution, alarmed at the light and air suddenly let in upon their immemorial habits and habitations, I discovered what appeared to be an inscription very rudely cut; and scraping off the soil I slowly spelt out the two words, *Dibus viteribus*. 'To the gods of old,' I was forced to translate it, in spite of the shock to my dim memories of grammar, and it was a comfort to reflect that the faithful and believing soldier who had scratched that dedication on the stone had escaped the smarting penalty he would have received if he had shown up such a specimen of Latin in one of our public schools.

A little further up the hillside I was confronted by a wall which from its solid breadth and the regularity of its squared stones I knew must be that hedge of Empire, the great barrier itself. Like the Great Wall of China, it could be seen far away running up hill and down, and at the dangerous gaps it was marked by square fortresses. At this spot it had been built within a few yards of the very edge of the cliff, and climbing over its broad and grass-grown top, I could look far below through tufts of fern and holly and mountain ash, barely rooted in crannies of the precipitous rock, right down upon a reedy lake, over the clear centre of which coots were bobbing their white-shielded heads, and expressing their satisfaction with things as they are in cries like the creaking of cart wheels. Northward, the moorland lay stretched out, still and untenanted under the immense air, like a brown and heaving sea, with broken crests against the horizon's rim. Behind me the autumn sun drove slowly down the west, and now and then a great bee or purple beetle lumbered comfortably over the Wall, booming his 'cello note, to find himself next moment hanging high in empty space above the inhospitable water, perturbed as an alderman who has blundered eastward of Aldgate Pump at the hour of lunch.

No human thing was in sight, except that far away up the straight old road I could just make out two little figures, like laborious ants, dragging some heavy burden along. It looked like a barrel-organ, and I vaguely wondered what they might be doing with it so far from the dancing slums. But soon forgetting them, I fell to imagining the day when at last Rome drew in her shortened arm, and the legions left their watch-fires to smoulder out upon that cliff, and across

A PRIESTESS TO APOLLO

the moor in front the savages came creeping until they climbed the wall and cautiously entered the deserted forts and peered along the empty streets of that very town, gazing upon the statues of gods with the awe of those who found the senators silent in the Forum. In marble's language they would read the dedications of altars to the Arcadian Pan and to the Apollo of Delphi. They felt no qualms about the grammar of *Dibus viteribus*. They felt no pity if they deciphered the little tombstone of Aurelia Quartilla, whose only history was that she lived thirteen years, five months, and twenty-two days, as I had myself read in the Newcastle museum. And now the abyss of time had swallowed savages and gods, together with the love which so carefully reckoned Aurelia's life, and nothing of them all was left but those few stones for antiquarians to germanise over.

Such ineffectual musings were suddenly scattered by the sweet minor of the popular song, beginning, 'Again the cricket wakes to sing.' Turning my head quickly, I beheld a sight strangely out of keeping with the surroundings. Near the eastern gate of that old Roman town an Italian organ-grinder was rolling out the tune with an air of concentrated fervour very different from the aristocratic unconcern of his class: and on a level space in front of him a slender girl, very poorly clad, was dancing in time to the regular beat of the music. At first I thought she danced the London mode, which, being Semitic in origin, is perhaps the same as pleased King Herod. But I saw that in her was more restraint and art, and that at definite pauses her upturned palms were raised towards the sun. Nine times the tune was repeated, and nine times, without variation, the girl went through her dance. Then the music stopped, and together they dragged the organ close up to the wall beside me.

'I don't know why it is, dear,' I heard her say, 'but it seems as if I could go on dancing for ever out here; only we must be careful of the instrument, and your time is not quite perfect.'

'Do not fret, sweet emblem of eternity,' answered the man. 'I hope to learn the organ's ways in the course of years. They can hardly be more difficult than woman's, I suppose. And, as the wise man said, I would fain grow old learning many things.'

I looked and saw the wild god's eyes, sad and appealing as a dog's, and over all his half-brutish features the sweet human smile, illumining sorrow, or defying it.

'Dear Pan, you are far from your Arcadian home,' I said, when they had climbed the wall and sat down to rest beside me.

'As far,' he replied, 'as a lover's heart from his far-off mistress, and no further. But in recognising me you pay yourself a fine compliment; for the poet says it is hard for a man to know the gods by sight, but the gods are known to each other.'

'Will you tell me,' I asked, 'why it is that you are here?'

'You see,' he answered, 'there is as yet no Pauper Immigration Act to exclude gods who have come down a little in the world; so that I was able to visit these regions in obedience to a command. You will think me very old-fashioned for practising obedience instead of praising it as an excellent thing for others, especially for the poor. But I'm afraid I was born a little old-fashioned, and I find obedience the only virtue pleasant in itself to practise. Every lover, at all events, declares that he would rather be a slave than free, if the beloved were his mistress.'

'But in obedience to what command,' I asked, 'do you bring a piano-organ out into the moors?'

'A voice,' he replied, 'kept repeating in my ears the warning—"Do not forget the god." Now, I myself at one time sent a similar message to the Athenians, and being still mindful of the pain of neglect, I was sorry to think that the god should be suffering from any neglect of mine, especially as he had always been so much my superior both in intellect and character. So for a long time I wondered how best I could comfort him by assurance of my piety, till at last I remembered that the Philosopher also kept hearing a warning voice, which commanded him to cultivate the Muses; and after he was sentenced to death, rather than leave the world without having obeyed the voice, he set to and made poetry, turning Æsop into verse, though he had but a day or so more to live, and most people would have thought it hardly worth while just before their execution to begin the practice of an art upon which the poets are said to spend a good deal of time, and not always to very good purpose. Anxious, therefore, not to be surpassed in piety even by a philosopher, I cast about whether I might not serve the god in some similar manner. For I had heard that service is strength, and were I weak as water I would rather be poured into a serviceable cup than slopped about at random.'

'But what form of service,' I asked, 'is possible with a barrel-organ in the desert?'

'In towns,' he answered, 'where people are so clever and so ready to exercise their gifts for the improvement of others, I feared that my homely strains would be scorned. But just as a man can always get plenty of love by paying his court to women whom no one else will notice, I thought I could best serve the god among people for whose welfare there is little artistic or philanthropic competition. And it seemed to me possible that in this solitude I might perhaps find some one who had escaped having good done to him, and so would be ready to welcome me. As to the organ, I hoped the god would consider it an advance from my own reedy pipings towards the music of the harp, by which the poets tell us he introduces peaceful law into the soul; and certainly the harp used to be of real service as medicine in the olden time. This piano-organ, at any rate, is the nearest approach to it which I can master—if indeed I may call myself master of it—and there is no knowing what its effect might be upon mental invalids. But I will not deny that at first the task appeared to me distasteful. Educated persons have bestowed much pity upon Apollo for having to tend flocks for the shepherd-king Admetus. But no one reflects how much more pitiful it would have been for Admetus to have to serve Apollo, fooling his time away on music and things of the mind when he wanted to be following the ewes great with young. Might it not in this sense be true that, as one of your own priests said, religion is a good servant but a bad master?'

'Then why, beloved god,' I said, 'did you take up the service at all?'

'Nay,' he answered, smiling; 'never ask me for reasons. A watched pot never boils, you know; and it was a wise law in Sparta which compelled even married lovers to see each other only by stealth. And so, keeping a warm and secret heart, I will bid you now farewell.'

'Oh, don't go yet,' said the girl sleepily, for she had stretched herself full length upon the tufted grass between us. 'To be here with you is the divine deliverance you speak of so often. And I think the mountains were at some time my home, for each looks as though he knew me and wondered what had happened to me all these years.'

'Let sleeping women lie,' said the god,

smiling again; 'and to that end, I will tell you a sleepy vision which was in a manner the direct cause of my presence here. When first those warning voices came, I was sullen as a lover who is not jealous indeed, but is humbled at the thought that in some respect his service must have fallen short, since his mistress needs the aid or converse of others than himself. Why should my worshippers wish for any help but mine? In what, I thought to myself, is the hand of the harp-player more skilled than the hand of the sower who delicately scatters his grain? Did not Xenophon himself say that kneading dough and shaking up beds and arranging pots and pans were movements as beautiful as a religious or cultivated dance, and that the inside of a Phœnician ship showed method and order more truly musical than the works of recent musicians? The Spartan king would not turn aside to hear a man imitate a nightingale to perfection, for he had heard the nightingale herself. The ploughboy, at whose coming the old cart-horse pricks his ears and breathes delight down his nostrils, knows more about the horse than all the artists, poets, and professors. To speak of such a man as uneducated is as absurd as to instruct a savage by means of stuffed specimens of his country's beasts in a museum. Seeing, therefore, that many were engaged in such arts, and more in talking upon them with airs of great solemnity, I turned in wrath from man as being a dull and frivolous creature, like all grown-up people in the eyes of children, and I took refuge with mice and little birds and unseen lilies, which belong to a nobler order of existence than man; for they do not whine over unreal fictions and lament surroundings too harsh for their sensitive souls, but live in self-sufficient joy and struggle, and die without obituary notices.

'But as I roamed, full of injured rage, the shade of the Great Mother herself stood before me, and she smiled through sadness, as when she sat in sorrow by the well at Eleusis, and smiled at Iambe's merry words; for the girl, you remember, was bright as a young doe in the fields, and her hair danced like daffodils upon the wind. Then she stroked me with her hand, and said, "Dear and trusty Dog-of-all-work, like the Pythagoreans I would bid you neither eat your heart nor poke the fire with your sword. Be not righteous overmuch, but condescend to consider yet again those humble souls over whom I gave you charge—if, indeed, we may be allowed to call them souls at all. You will find in nearly all of them one very strange desire and delight, reaching far back to those remote wells of being from which you yourself are sprung. For you surely remember the somewhat primitive monsters which were your childhood's play mates — winged crocodiles and serpentining kangaroos and elephants with fins and plashing feet. Did they not solace a yearning in their hearts with dragon cat-calls and trumpetings from giraffe-like necks, resounding merrily over the sluggish ooze where now they lie coldly embedded, and give no sign of all that wild desire for something they hardly knew what — something hardly compatible, one would have supposed, with their grotesque and earthly forms? And in these present days, when the world has grown gentle and mature, the spider yet takes a pleasure in tapping his tail hour after hour upon a patch of hollow wood. The death-watch beetle, active leaper though he be, stands still a whole night through just for the joy of listening to the click of his jerking neck; for it seems he gets no extra pleasure from the terrors of maids and lubber hinds upon their straw. For his own delight the cricket with repeated chirp makes night companionable to the wanderer from farm to farm. The bittern and the snipe drum and boom from the darkening fen. At supreme moments of a lover's night the night-jar sounds a higher and tenderer note, and claps his soft wings like muffled cymbals above his back. The slug-eating savage drubs his tom-tom till he faints in unimagined ecstasy. At the thud and rumble of a stick on a dried skin every brave heart throbs with double valour. And even Æschylus, who fought by your side at Marathon, and rightly ordered that his presence in the battle should be the only fact engraved upon his tomb, spent much of his life in making poetry. If, then, in all these charges of yours there is found some common desire, some common delight, it must be impossible for you to remain indifferent to it, or contemptuous."

'"Impossible, certainly, dear lady," I answered, "for I may be called a lover of my worshippers, and lovers say that to them the whole of the beloved's nature is entirely lovable, nor can anything in it be thought of as common or unclean."

'"But this strange quality of which I speak," she continued, "is said to be due to the promptings of the god, and without it those charges of ours might, perhaps, too readily fall under the tyranny of inert flesh, like the Cyclops who sacrificed only to himself and to his belly, which was in his opinion the greatest of the gods. If, therefore, the gift of the god helps to save them from a swinish ease, lest the brief generations of living things should die in their own fat, like the flame of overladen candles, and pass into their long sleep before they are well awake, I entreat you to listen to the warning voice, and not to blaspheme, but serve. For I would that all my creatures were quick in spirit, tempered like deer-hounds straining at the start. If the god's power, then, can help to this end, let us beseech his favour that the words and deeds of our worshippers may be arranged as the notes of the true Dorian mood, that raises men to the better part of discretion, which, as you know, is valour; and being Dorian, the mood, no doubt, is Apollo's own."

'That is what my mistress, the Great Mother, said,' continued the sunburnt deity; 'and now whenever I meet the express followers of the god passing through life with that solemn aloofness of theirs, like cranes stalking through a poultry-yard, so that I am overcome by the grandeur of their words and appearance, I find a reassuring comfort in the thought that even common and innocent creatures of my own, such as spiders, beetles, and crickets, are touched by a similar spirit, being, as it seems, in some degree inspired also by the god. To my ignorance, of course, many mysteries remain impenetrable—mysteries of the sphere in which critics and philosophers and poets and musicians habitually move; but being unwilling to blaspheme like an ill-bred dog which goes sniffing about a sanctuary, I have determined to do what best service I could with this humble instrument. So, taking this strange girl to bear me company, I came first to the place where you saw her dancing just now. For it was the site of a shrine to the god, erected by a Roman cohort in obedience to Apollo himself, speaking from Claros on the Ephesian bay. And perhaps the god's divinity still lingers there, though his service was early corrupted into the mystical worship of Mithras by one of those clouds of insanity which from age to age sweep up from the bewildered East, confusing the mind till it sees the god's power in signs and miracles rather than in the daily glory of light and joy. But indeed, sir, upon such dim themes you must suffer me to be silent. My concern is with this ancient little world, and a world in the hand is worth two in the nebula. Besides, as you know, I never could make a long speech without putting on a veil—like a politician, except that I wear the veil visibly over my face.'

We sat silent for a time, looking towards the haunted Borderland, whilst the girl slept upon the grass.

'Dear beast and god,' I said at last, 'I fear that in professing obedience to Apollo you are but beguiling me. For he died long ago, and his temples are ruined. I have read that one of the latest of the Pythian prophetesses was a poor peasant's daughter, pure and beautiful, but unlearned as your companion there. And when she was set upon the tripod, and the pilgrims stood outside awaiting her responses, she refused to prophesy to them, but remained dumb as a statue. When at last she spoke, her voice was wild and incomprehensible, and her body writhed like a ship tormented by the wind. Then, to the terror of priests and pilgrims alike, she shrieked and fell, and when they ventured to return they found her prostrate as the dead. A few days after, it was given out that she had actually died, being too frail to bear the inrush of the god. But others said that Apollo had made her an immortal wanderer for ever, like that earliest Pythian, whose face is still seen upon the wandering moon. That peasant girl, at any rate, was one of the last priestesses of whom we have a definite account; and when, a few generations later, the Apostate sent Oribasius, his physician and quæstor, to restore the temple, it was no priestess, but the dying voice of the god himself which was heard—then for the last time in all this world—crying with calm lamentation:

"Go, tell the king, to earth the dædal house
 Has fallen, and no longer Phœbus owns
 His hidden cell or his prophetic bays
 Or murmuring spring; the murmuring spring is
  hush'd."'

I had hardly finished the well-known lines when the girl moved in her sleep, smiling like one who slowly wakes and feels he has a hidden joy at heart, but does not yet remember what it is. 'Apollo! King Apollo!' she cried. Full of astonishment, I saw her eyes open and become fixed upon the blue above her. Under the soiled and worn points of her cotton bodice her breasts heaved like the Sibyl's. 'Apollo! King Apollo!' came the old Greek cry again, and then like a dim memory which unexpectedly flits across the mind and is gone, followed her sudden story of the past.

'It was early morning,' she said, 'and the air was cold. High up above me the twin peaks of the mountain only just glimmered with snow under the rising light. The night was still dark in the laurels at the mountain's foot, where the gorge divides the cliff, and the cypress at the turn of the road coming up from the plain could hardly yet be seen. But the smoke of myrrh was already rising from the temple itself, and the god's servants moved about like shades among the columns, sprinkling water from the holy stream, and sweeping off the dust of yesterday with olive boughs. Others scared the birds from the roof with cries and arrows. I stood by the entrance-door and waited, looking towards my father's farm, where the cows would now be calling from the byre. It was only three days since the priest came while I was milking, and summoned me to be the priestess to the god. But unwillingly I changed my clothes and went with them, crying along the road at the thought of leaving my father and mother and the cattle and goats, who all unwillingly saw me go. Therefore now I looked towards my home till the light crept down the waterfalls of the Gleaming Crags, and soon I could see the divine forms fixed upon the temple—the strong man ridding the world of monsters, and Pallas laying the giants low, and King Apollo himself. And the shields hanging above the columns sounded faintly, like bronze bells in the morning wind. But the inner shrine was covered up with curtains, and Heaven was woven upon them, gathering all his stars. There was Night, and the Pleiades, and the Sailors' Guides, and Orion with his sword, and Arctus twisting the sky round the Pole. And on the ground in the midst of the sanctuary lay the great white stone, the centre of the earth, crowned with flowers, and Gorgons watch over it for ever. The sacred roads from all the ends of the world lead to it, and they are at peace for ever.

'Then I saw a band of sacred envoys coming down the road cleft through the mountains from the east, for Athens had sent them, since watchers on the Acropolis had seen the summer lightning give the sign above Mount Parnes. Pilgrims were coming, too, up from the sea, making their way into the mountains across the consecrated plain, where they had put to shore after long voyages from islands and unknown promontories. On the temple's altar the sacrifices of frankincense and corn and mallows were now made ready, and in my hands were placed the laurel-leaves and barley, and water from the sacred spring. Then I was made to eat and drink of them, standing beside the entrance of the deep chasm where the vapour issues from the heart of the prophetic Earth. And outside I could hear the pilgrims talking together, and telling each other the reasons why they had come. Most of them were poor country people like us, shepherds who had paid a lamb for the journey and fishermen who had sailed to the god in their own little boats. And their questions were about the barren wife or the erring son, or the oppression of the rich. For the god could strike, but was pitiful, and could

A PRIESTESS TO APOLLO

heal. From age to age he had governed kings and taught wisdom to the wise, and yet in this very temple he had said that he knew the number of the sand and the measure of the sea, and understood the dumb, and gave ear to him that speaketh not. Surely, then, he, if any, would listen to the silent crying of the poor. So they spoke among themselves, telling the reasons why they had come, and the answer to all their fears and doubts was to be uttered by me.

'Suddenly I heard new footsteps, and the inmost recess was opened and I was led in, full of fear. I saw the bottomless chasm and the breath of the prophetic Earth rising from it. A seat of bronze stood over the chasm, half covered in the smoke, and I was set upon it and left alone to wait for the coming of the god. Still I heard the questions and prayers for guidance ringing in my ears, but, covering my face with my hands, I waited, for I was afraid. And how should I speak wisdom to the poor, I who was a poor maid and nothing? So astonishment held me silent, and I waited for the god.

'Long I waited and there was no sign, but the outlines of the columns around me began to shiver and fade, as though a grey darkness were stealing in. I shut my eyes in terror that something would befall, and waited in such silence that I heard my blood leaping with expectation. Suddenly on the silence came a low wail of sorrow, and I knew it for what it was—the cry of a mother over the erring son, when she saw him netted and transfixed upon the arena of a far-off city, while row upon row of spectators shouted applause. Quickly there came another cry, as of mingled joy and anguish, and I knew that a woman in a mountain hut of Lacedæmon had borne a son, so fruitful had been the shepherd's visit to the god. After that cry, a gasp, hardly audible upon the air, shivered through the sanctuary, and I saw the rich oppressor lying upon his bed, his legs drawn up in pain beneath the lion's skin; the purple hangings of the door just moved, and some one was creeping out. Then came the voice of the lover wandering far away unsatisfied, but ever drawing closer, and the whispered supplications of the belovèd, longing no less than he, till with hardly time for one low sound heart lay on heart. I heard the shout of fighting men, the clash of their swords, the short, hard breathing of things upon the edge of life, and the low sob like a child's as the iron plunged into their flesh. And afterwards came the voice of a shepherd calling to his flock up the deep gorge of Pindus where the black ilex grows. With his cries the sound of a pipe was mingled; it had but three notes, but ah! with what sweetness its music filled the air, telling of peace and sunny weather. But joy was broken by the thud of drums, and I beheld the hosts of Ethiopia beating the ground with black and naked feet. In the face of the moon they shook the lance, and the ground was staked out with the heads of their enemies. Again I heard the sound of dancing, and saw a cleared circle among pines beside a northern sea; and on it danced a girl, her black hair whirling like a driven cloud; the brass and silver of her armlets jangled together; from the onlookers, swaying with her form, the jangle of innumerable brass and silver arose, and above it shrilled the panting and long-drawn sighs of many lutes. Quicker and quicker grew the dance; the spotted furs rose and fell around the wild girl's limbs; the blaze of wooden logs turned her to crimson; she flickered like a tongue of flame upon the ground. Then the grey mists fell, and I beheld long lines of speechless men, moving solemnly through a land like thin grey snakes; they came from victorious war, but on a broad iron shield in front of them they carried their leader dead. With horns and muffled drums they told their deep-toned sorrow to the clouds. Then rose the triumph of long trumpets sounding together, note after note, and all with one blare of glory; and I saw long processions of white-robed priests moving towards a white temple upon a promontory, and praising the god with song and music as they went. But after the trumpets I heard the sighing of a free but vanquished people, and their low cries of anguish and defiance as the conqueror stamped them into the burnt and bloodstained ground, while now and then one among them would raise the thin echo of the songs they used to sing when freedom was theirs.

'So I listened and gazed, while scene after scene upon the world's face passed before me, and I seemed to understand the voice of all joy and sorrow, from the singing of the little child who follows the cows down hill, to the lamentations of Asia over the Great King dead. Like strands in the interwoven work of the loom the voices of men and women sounded amid the cries of birds and beasts, the wailing of the wind, the rustle of trees, and the gulp and reiteration of the sea. So that the whole earth seemed to utter a music of pleasure and pain, as she swung beneath the bridge of the Milky Way. Whether that music is heard at all by the moon and nearer stars, or whether the earth appears to them dumb as a dolphin, which loves melody indeed, but cannot sing—what prophet is wise enough to tell? But I could hear it, for the god granted me power; and at the sound of all that sadness and desire I was overcome as by the voice of Destiny, which Zeus himself obeys. And as the music grew I heard the far-off footsteps of the god, so that in wonder I cried aloud, and falling prone upon the steps of the shrine I saw the temple and the inrushing people but for a moment, nor ever again thereafter, for the god took me to himself that I might be his handmaid in many lands.'

Her voice suddenly ceased, and her eyes were closed again. For a while the cross-bred god and I watched her as she lay between us.

'It seems,' he said at last, 'that the god has again borne her from the world, like a dream on wings which follow down the ways of sleep. But her presence here proves it was rather rash of you to speak of the god as dead. For we must suppose him at least as long-lived as a being to whom he gave immortality. And you will remember besides that a god lives exactly as long as he has worshippers; nor can we refuse the title of worshipper to the priestess, though she was but a peasant girl. If, then, he be still alive, may we without impiety inquire what would be his abiding function in this our time?'

'To you the search would be of special interest,' I replied; 'for I remember an old, old story that you yourself were Apollo's first teacher in music on the plains where Troy was afterwards to stand. It is a significant tale.'

'Oh, sir,' said the god modestly, 'spare me the schoolmaster's reflected glory—a sad consolation at the best, especially when he has been so far surpassed by his pupil. But let us rather resume the god's attributes in brief, so that we may the more easily recognise him, should we meet with any trace of his power. He was born late in time, you remember, and after long throes of anguish, foreshadowing the toil of the wise. The unmoving world would not receive him, but a floating island of adventure was his cradle. Delos was its name among men, but the poet heard the gods call it the shining star on earth's black round. For, from his birth up, the god, like rising light, did battle against the shadows and spectres which crowd the poor bewildered mind with false shapes of hope and fear. And because he was the enemy of all that is vague and distorted, it was to his radiance that the maddened penitent turned, when dogged by the shapeless phantoms of memory and remorse, childless children of the night, which sit beside the wakeful pillow; and to him the Cretan prophet prayed, summoned to dispel the unreal terrors which brooded over Athens, when her gods had turned away because of her cruel sin.

'And it appears that Apollo's mode of reassuring the mind and purging it of its self-created tormentors, was an exercise of mind and body by which the senses became awake to the definite forms of beauty, rejecting all that is chaotic and vague. And by this art of his he converted the shocks and blows of earth into a music of song and march, which to the hearing ear brought with it the inestimable benefit of happiness. For he who caught the sound of that harmony in word or music, though it might be the sorrowful utterance of some voice crying in the wilderness of a city's wealth, was at once pervaded with joy and went forward with fresh courage, like a soldier who hears his comrade calling to him far off among the enemy. His sight was renewed, and to him the world was transfigured with truth, so that he perceived what had hitherto lain unseen before his eyes, and the earth looked fresh again like the new moon, or, as the Italians say, like a mouth that is kissed. I suppose it is because they sometimes have a share in this divine power of renewing and revealing the old world that poets and writers and people of that sort have often been tolerated among serious, warlike, and hard-working people. Do you not think that may be the reason?

'At any rate, I have been told that he who really heard the god's word was raised to a higher state than his nature seemed to promise; just as real lovers are much better people when they are together, being full of unwonted generosity and a courage that will go through fire. From such a man's soul the word of the god drove the dull passions which go to their satisfaction half-hearted and sleepy, like tame and hireling animals, and, instead of watching at each turn for the guide-posts of conduct, he strenuously followed those inner counsels of perfection which are the god's tables of commandments. Nations, even from a distance, have been drawn by the apparition of those rare flames in the dark, and have been encouraged by the very thought of their presence in the common life. They have listened to them as to the oracles of the god himself, for by word and deed such followers of his presented to the soul a world which seemed like its native home. They revealed to the heart its forgotten secrets, as music sometimes may, and gave it the peace of energy fulfilled. Communing with them, man rose to an unaccustomed but natural height, from which the true value of things was manifest, so that, like the god himself, he could enter, lightly but securely armed, into the contest with the Pythons and other dreary spirits which cried and ravaged around the mountain's base.

'If then,' the pastoral deity continued, in a very cheerful tone, 'the power of the god has really been of this nature in the past; and if, as seems likely, he is still able to give succour, perhaps I was right in listening to the voice which warned me not to forget him. At any rate, I would willingly serve him to the best of my skill, in the spirit of that blind old Spartan who compelled his friends to lead him into the thick of the battle, exclaiming, "At least I shall do to blunt an enemy's sword!"'

'And for such service,' I said, 'your barrel-organ is no doubt sufficient.'

'More than sufficient,' he answered, 'if only I could play it really well. But as we are so close to the god's altar here, perhaps you would allow me to offer up a brief prayer before we go. With your permission, then, I would pray the god to keep my mind from phantoms and from hesitation and from half-desires. A god of such high powers is surely able to grant such simple petitions as those. But for me they would be quite enough to ask, and so I may be silent now. Words on horseback, you know, were always far beyond my power.

'But awake, my beloved of the kindred earth! Your knowledge of the god is surely greater than mine. Once more allow the organ's handle to kiss the tender inward of your hand, that having played another tune to his honour we may set out upon our way. For indeed I am as hungry as the grasshoppers when they starved themselves to death in their delight at listening to the Muses' song.'

The air she played was another simple music-hall melody, such vulgar and tavern music as, in Sir Thomas Browne's words, makes one man merry, another mad, but struck in him a deep fit of devotion and a profound contemplation of the first composer. When it was finished they turned westward, bidding me farewell, and the edge of the horizon, as the earth revolved, hid them and the sun together. Then the ways were darkened, and all the stars shone out, so that the shepherd's heart was glad.

III

THE FIRE OF PROMETHEUS

Through the long noon, while the sun marched as usual across the enormous sky—through the dead hours of the day, when thunder fell upon us like blows, and the lightning's white arm could hardly pierce the shrieking columns of the rain, I lay upon the mountain-side among the soldiers of a large army. In war, as in extreme grief, a numbness overcomes the spirit; the mind swoons under the stress of anxiety or pain; it can feel no more, and can realise no more. Situations which at other times would appear to it incredible and dreamlike with terror, are then quite natural, as though they came in the ordinary course. Horror, astonishment, the realisation of the truth—these are things that grow up afterwards, but for the time, perception and even fear are stifled by something, which is perhaps their own excess. My chief thought was a weary longing for the night. When would the night come to shelter us from that other shrieking storm which swept across the woof of drenching water? When would it come to lull that other thunder which rattled and paused and was renewed and died away and roared again with quickened rage as though in mortal haste for our destruction? Hour after hour I lay, peering vainly into the chaos of rain and lightning and invisible peril, while around me the air sang and growled with lead, and men died. The fate of an army, the issue of a war, depended on the mountain ridge where I was lying, and of such advantages as an attacking force can hold, the enemy had all. Yet I no more considered defeat than did the gods when

THE FIRE OF PROMETHEUS 87

the Titans set about their assault upon heaven, and the men around me seemed to realise no more than myself either the importance of the struggle or its meaning to themselves.

Food, drink, and the coming night that would end our danger—those were the things we thought of; and among the coarse grass and rocks on which we lay, beetles and ants were hurrying up and down, seeking escape from the stormy rivulets of the rain.

Night came at last. Somewhere behind that whirling curtain of storm and war, the sun departed to light the tinkling lines of muleteers up quiet gorges of the Andes. Renewed now and again in spitting outbursts like the end of angry words, the firing slackened. In the gathering darkness, forms of unusual size began to move about. Men got up from invisible hiding-places and shook themselves, as though shaking off the fear of death. With just the same interest they tried to rub the slime from their knees. They spat, and turned their heads, and looked at each other. One or two whispered something, as people whisper in church or at a funeral. An officer came by, trying to walk as usual. He contrived to speak aloud after a few attempts, and fire and thunder mixed never fell on us with so strange a shock as the sound of his voice. The men watched him go as ghosts might watch a fellow-ghost in limbo, and his word of command was passed almost silently from mouth to mouth.

Tormented by thirst, I turned and scrambled down the hill to the narrow road which in peace time had led from one little village to another far away across the position we were defending. A mere track of loose stones and mud, it was now choked from end to end by all the chaos which eddies behind the course of battle: the wounded on stretchers dripping red, the wounded in carts, the wounded tottering back on their own feet, sobbing as they went; ammunition wagons with terrified and screaming mules; batteries taking position in reserve; dying horses being urged out of the way with whips and bayonets; broken-down limbers; reinforcements in companies threading their way to the front; orderlies trying in vain to gallop through the muddle of it all. Splashing along the gutter which the rain had washed beside the road, I got among the scattered houses at last. Nearly all were dark and empty, but from the main church as I passed it came the cries of the wounded and the quiet hum of surgeons and attendants at their work. It had been suddenly turned into a hospital. Lights were burning inside, and cast the crimsons and golds of the stained windows upon the steaming, misty air. I don't know why the sight of those colours affected me so strangely then. Hunger and exhaustion may have given distinctness to the vision they called up, but to most people the outside of a lighted church at night is full of half-forgotten associations, and one of a child's first mysteries is the enchanted brilliance of the windows as he leaves the porch to the sound of the organ's voluntary.

In the midst of all the pain and wretchedness, there came to me the smell of an evening in early spring; and instead of the crowded and slushy track between the bare rock and the starveling houses appeared a gentle, gravelly road, guided by clipped hedgerows through plough and pasture from which a god could have scraped the fatted soil as a thrifty nurse scrapes off the children's butter. The horses waiting with the squire's carriage were like the land, their shining quarters all coated over with laps and folds of fatness. So were the congregation, who, having sung 'A few more years shall roll,' and prayed to be led

THE FIRE OF PROMETHEUS

through the desert here, came out of the church door, well clothed, well washed, well fed. Like the Ancient Mariner watching the water-snakes at play, I blessed them unaware. All had come to the service warmed and enlivened by their tea, and were now returning to supper with Sunday night's exhilaration of duty performed and tongues released from religious silence, whilst the collection-plate tinkled at the door. Issuing into blue air from the bright orange of the porch, lover signalled to lover under a silver star. So the ghostly but substantial procession passed out into a land of bread and flesh and milk and drinkable water, secure of the morrow, and rooted in a past of uninterrupted days. As I watched them move comfortably down the poignant ways of memory, I knew that an exactly similar procession would be crossing that ancient porch to-night (for it was Sunday); lovers would signal their meetings in the darkened lanes, the smell of violets would swim like dreams through the air, and from the fields the lambs cry sleepily. I wondered how it was possible for those people ever to be unhappy in their nestling homes. No misery seemed to count beside the wretchedness of war, and a longing for peace and all that peace means came over me. I longed for the tranquillity of the country lanes and the purple woods of spring; I longed for the spacious and quiet homes, for the silver smiling on the tablecloth and on the darkly gleaming sideboards, for the soft stir of women in the room and the faint smell of their hair and dresses, for the talking and quick laughter, for the clean sheets on wholesome beds, and the glad calling of the rooks when morning came above the elms.

In a dark and empty shed which was now my home, I drank deep of a bucket into which the rain was dripping through the roof, and began eating my half

THE FIRE OF PROMETHEUS 93

biscuit, very slowly, to make it last. I was full of vague and bitter rage—rage at the grit and sand in the biscuit, at the slimy floor and the sopping rug under which I had to sleep—rage at the risk of death, which might prevent me seeing anything I loved again. I prayed to witness the enemy's quick and entire overthrow, to watch them scattered over the hills and swept from the plains by our pursuing guns. Only over their dead could we win the road to happiness, and now they were actually attacking us, and on the rocks our dead lay almost as thick as theirs. It seemed as though a natural law had gone crazy. Full of irritation and angry fears of what the night would bring to succeed so horrible a day, I fell asleep with exhaustion, while a thin dust of water kept stealing down on me through the chinks of the boarding.

Hours passed before I woke, and then the rain had stopped and there was no more noise of wagons on the road. 'Now is the time they'll renew the attack,' I said wearily to myself; and getting up from the filthy ground I went out again into the night and wandered back towards a part of the front where I had not been before, though it was a continuation of the same ridge which we had been defending. All was quiet now. Here and there I came upon little groups of our men along the line, stretched in sleep or huddled together for warmth, though the night was hot. Late and red the waning moon had risen, and it now gave an uncertain light, crossed by mists and films of moving cloud, the rear-guard of the storm. Stumbling over the rocks, I reached the further crest of the hill, where sentries were posted at intervals, and from there I could see down into the misty valley along which the enemy had come. Ridge after ridge of mountain stretched before me just discernible in the moonlight, and all looked so free and peaceful that war seemed an absurdity, and with the mere desire of escape, as from an iron ring, I began to creep down the steep hillside. The dead ground soon concealed me from above, and I there sat down to brood and to await what might happen before the dawn.

I waited long in the silence, and then I suddenly heard something like the gentle movement of a shy animal, and looking to the side I saw a figure stooping down over a dark object lying upon the ground. The figure appeared to be shaking a man by the shoulder as though to wake him up. I got my revolver ready in my hand, but uncertain whether it might not be one of our own sentries, I first said in a low voice, 'Hullo, there! Why can't you let the poor fellow sleep?'

'I'm afraid I must,' said the other without looking up: 'yet it is but ten pulses of the blood since he was awake.'

Sitting down, he raised the man's head and supported it on his knees, as gently as a woman moves her sleeping lover. I went and peered into the motionless face. Under the dim moon it was a blur of greenish white, like the moon herself.

'Why, he's one of the enemy!' I said, seeing the badge on his cap.

'No,' the other answered; 'he is dead.' He took the man's hand, and one by one undid the tightly clenched fingers, stretching them out and watching them slowly curl together again.

'Look,' he said, 'touch this queer thing, and you will find it still warmish and limp. Only sixty pulses of the blood ago it was awake with life. See what peculiar stuff it is, solid and yet full of red and blue waters which have only just stopped running backwards and forwards—oh, far quicker than the waves upon a shore; a network substance of tender cords and jellies, finer than the

THE FIRE OF PROMETHEUS 97

loom, covered with a porous coating, more pliant than silk, and fitting closer than a light lady's robe. Five hooks, you see, with props and sticks of hollowed lime, pulleys and hinges complete, and tipped with horn. And all alive—"all but alive" still, as the honest fishmongers say—only three minutes ago quivering with the last beat of life. Only this morning it buttoned this jacket, or carried food to this poor mouth, just as the life devised, and far better than any contrivance man has ever made. But now nothing can set it moving ever again. I tried to hold in the life and keep it mingled with the body, I tried to catch it by the throat and prevent its escape. But while I clutched it tight, it was gone through my fingers. To feel it go was worse than a lover's longing which vanishes in waking. For the life had been there, and now it was not anywhere at all.'

'Many things are sad, but death is
G

not the saddest, and the poor fellow is only dead,' I said, speaking like the chorus of a play.

'You are young compared to me, and therefore wise,' he answered. 'But this rough hand, now more perishable than a stone—what astonishing things it has done since it was pink and small, pressing against some mother's breast. Now it is lined and twisted and embrowned, just like a wild hawk's claw. Year after year it has harnessed the horse and ox, and scraped the mud from their coated fur. It has cloven the woods for fire and dug trenches where water should run. Inside it is hard and knotted with the plough and spade. It has shorn the wool from sheep, and flung the seeds of corn trustfully upon the earth. It has shovelled snow from the cottage door. It has heaped a road across the swampy fen. Steeped in filth, and caked with dust that clave to its sweat, it has seemed but a clod of earth, more insensible than the cloven feet of oxen. Yet it has known pleasure better than the marble hands of gods. At the fire it has warmed itself, and after the heat of the day it has held the wine. It has touched the hands of other men, and stroked the lamb's-wool hair of children, and carried them along the weary road. Do you not suppose that it too has very likely throbbed with ecstasy at the touch of the beloved? Has it not embraced her, and been laid upon her heart, feeling the bell of her life ring muffled in her softness? What has the King of Babylon's hand done more or better than this poor bit of cold and greenish stuff which already is falling back into the earth it knew so well? Yet all such things he cast behind him, and in the assault was with the first, although the last to die. As he lay unnoticed in this cranny of the rocks, scorched by the sun and sodden by the rain, he knew all day long that he should never see his little farm again, or wake at dawn, or hear the voice of any woman.'

'If he so valued his life,' I said, 'he should not have come out to battle.'

'Do you not value your life?' he answered. 'To him it was as sweet as to you. Do you wish never to see again the things and people you are fond of, or never again to do what most you like? It was for love of him that this coloured rag about his neck was made. He was among my worshippers; oh, why was he not content in all the good things I can give—in rising up and lying down, in love and pleasant food and all the deep laughter of the world? Now he lies here quenched. His beard and hair are matted with blood and water mixed, his clothes are rent into holes and coated with mud, his toes stick out through the fragments of his boots. What was it drove him on to leave his home and flocks and all he loved beside? In his heart there burned a raging fire.

The Titans possessed him, and now like a Titan he lies prone.'

'Poor fellow,' I said, 'he has met with a strange epitaph, who all his life was insignificant and unknown—now to be called a Titan when he is dead, and more insignificant still.'

'I admit,' he said, laughing, with a far-off look as though he were calling up scenes long hidden; 'I admit the outward resemblance is not very great. Dear and savage sons of earth, gigantic and uncouth, they wallowed in ocean, making it boil like a pot, and in their wrath or jollity they hurled mountains with all their trees from land to land. Black and red they were, and their fiery hair streamed upon the clouds as the sun went down in storm. With the sides of precipices they built their homes, and on beds of flat-topped hills they stretched their coiling limbs to rest, shaking their fists in exultation among the clouds when morning woke them.

The joints of behemoth were their food, and with pails of foaming milk they washed down the slices of leviathan. The passion of their love shook the earth like earthquakes of the prime.

'Suddenly fate came—fate with the limits that conquer all things but the thoughts and desires of the soul. High in heaven, above the topmost mountains, the trim, white gods appeared, and against their fastidious pride those earth-born monsters raged in vain, breathing out defiance, lifting their wild arms against the sky, piling up their mountains that the height of heaven might be scaled. The lightning blazed. On sea and land their bodies writhed. Before they could say "What is it?" the lightning blazed. Bolts of fire hissed in their fiery blood. Shrieking they lay as the tempest shrieks upon the cliffs when speeding over the sea it smites the armoured and creviced rocks with blow on blow, and to the thunder of the poles their roarings made answer. Precipices fell to cover them, and the weight of mountains hardly stilled the twistings of their pain. Solid beds of granite were molten with their rage. The crust of the world was turned to jelly. It rent and split, and through its chinks their nostrils breathed the sulphurous smoke of their anguish. Up from deep chasms they spat their boiling spittle against the sky. With their sighs they shot the depths of the sea aloft, so that weak water stood up straight upon a watery floor like the columns of the gods. Through their prisons of broad-based mountains their torturing fires burst the breathing-holes whence issued flame mixed with crags and fervent boulders and the melted water of adamantine ores. Day and night for ever the smoke of their misery hung upon the mountain-tops. Their crimson indignation scorched the cool grey clouds that fluttered past, and brought them to earth like birds transfixed. As often as they turned their weary sides, the world shook and the crystal pinnacles of the hills toppled into ruin. So sprawled across the face of earth they lay in lengths of bleeding cinder.'

He ceased, and drew the limbs of the dead man straight, removing some rough stones from beneath him, as though they could hurt him still. Then leaning over him, he sighed and said: 'The outward resemblance indeed is small; but though he is so far greater than all the Titans, his fate is much the same, and he has won a crown like theirs.'

'Your speech,' I said, 'is ever a journey varied by collisions.'

Looking up like simplicity surprised, he answered: 'But is it not a glorious crown to be well lamented? And the Titans, you know, had that advantage. Why, the whole circle of the world joined in lamentation for their ancient sovereignty—the days when things went merrily, though with some pleasing disorder. The dear Earth mourned over them, beweeping with bitter tears the pangs of children whose bones her young womb had formed. And did not the poet tell us that all who loved the wild young Earth mourned too—the wanderers of Asia, and those who pitch beside the lake at the world's edge, and the spearmen watching like eagles from the peaks above the gulf of nothingness. Was it not a crown of triumph to touch the hearts which none could tame—the breastless girls who lay the bow and not the baby to their side, and sweep across the desert, horse and limbs beclouded in their whirling hair? Or think of Atlas, upon whom fell the bitterest doom that can befall the damned—the doom of usefulness. Bound in steel, he propped the turning dome of heaven, and but for him the hosts of stars would have fluttered down upon the earth like twinkling snow. Yet the poet says:

> "For him the waves of the sea are heard
> Moaning in cadence, and the precipitous gulf
> Groans, and the black chasm of the unseen world
> Mutters its deep-hid woe;
> Yea, from the holy streams a pitying voice
> Whispers of sorrow as they brightly go."

Would you choose the acclamations of victory rather than be mourned like that? Crowns are of many kinds, and there are gods who linger with the weaker side. Let us therefore lament this man, as the Titans were lamented.'

'With all my heart,' I answered. 'But, after all, the Titans were ignorant and mistaken. The gods were against them.'

'Oh yes, I know,' he sighed; 'any one can see that now. There was one of them saw it at the time, and being neither ignorant nor mistaken himself, he even helped the gods. Yet in the end he fared no better for his foresight.

THE FIRE OF PROMETHEUS

There is a cliff in Caucasus. At its foot the innumerable waves are smiling. Above it moves the scorching sun, and darkness warps it with the frost. An eagle tears the heart that so loved mankind.'

As he spoke, he undid the dead man's filthy and torn shirt, and smoothed the dark hair on his chest, down which the blood had trickled.

'Here, indeed,' he said, 'the fire of Prometheus has gone out. But have you never thought of fire how strange it is, how it multiplies itself more quickly than lovers, more quickly than the jelly of the sea, which splits and is two? With even greater similitude to itself it produces its young; for in a moment a hundred flames may spring, yet each will be the same flame as the first and as every other. Even if the first goes out, it lives identical and unappeased in all the rest. Of the same nature is the fire of Prometheus. Here it has gone out, but who knows how many flames may already have sprung from it?—each the same as itself, or differing only in brightness or colour according to the heart in which it dwells.'

'I have heard,' I said, 'how the one intelligent Titan brought fire down from heaven to men, carrying it in a fennel-stalk, of all strange warming-pans, and how wofully he suffered for his philanthropic ways. But I suppose the fire you now speak of is something different?'

'I am hardly sure,' he answered, with his puzzled air. 'For I have seen this inner fire make the inside of a face reflect its flame, just as a blazing log reddens the outside. And when the inner fire dies away, the face turns to dull ashes, like burnt love-tokens. I have felt that if a heart in which this fire kindled, could suddenly be laid bare, bright tongues of flame would leap from it as from a forge blown by the bellows; and sometimes I have seen the very

THE FIRE OF PROMETHEUS

depths of human eyes turn crimson with little points of fire—more crimson than a hare's eye when you catch it sideways in the sun. So that I am inclined to think the inner and outer fires may originally have been the same, and now only differ in the stuff on which they feed. But if I am wrong, please laugh at my simplicity.'

'I think you yourself,' I said, 'are never far from laughter; but I cannot laugh to-night, being sorrowful.'

'Nay,' he answered, 'if you will not laugh, and are sorrowful enough for understanding, I might tell you a story, almost as short as strange, about that selfsame fire.

'You remember what the poet tells us about the race of poor little mortal men and women when first they began to venture out upon the scum which gathered over the boiling star of earth. It was still warm in parts and everywhere flexible, so that what to-day was a plain might to-morrow be tossed up into a snow-capped mountain, or sunk to a lake, full of bitumen and biting salts. That condition of things was enough by itself to give great uncertainty to existence, and upon this bewildering surface men crept about, astonished and at random, never knowing what might happen next, or in what altitude and surroundings they might wake in the morning. Understanding no guidance of stars or of seasons, they lived in shocks, as when we slide in sleep from catastrophe to catastrophe. So the poet, describing their condition, says:

"Seeing they saw not, in those ancient days,
   And hearing heard not, but like shapes of dreams,
   Their life was one long whirl of inconsequence."

'Of course they enjoyed no comforts of expensive simplicity such as you love. They did not even build sunny little houses, but for shelter from rain and heat they grubbed holes with their claws like phantom ants, or lay huddled together in slimy caverns where the roof dripped upon them till they steamed. In cold and damp and misery they lived, uncertain of the morrow, and they stayed their hunger by swallowing seeds and berries, or if they saw a four-footed animal sick and dying they crowded round him pelting him with stones, and then leapt upon his body with gluttonous howls, tearing his limbs asunder and gnawing them like lions; for they were not at all refined.

'But Prometheus, being only half a god, pitied their wretchedness, as he went among them to and fro from heaven. You know what strange services he did the poor creatures, for he himself described it all to those dear girls of the sea who came to cheer his lonely suffering with the sighs of their little bosoms and with commonplace as tender as their own caresses. Birds know the coming seasons, but poor man had to be taught their order by the punctual stars, which, as perhaps you may have heard, do not run about anyhow as they like, but have their risings and settings fitted with extreme nicety. Stars are, no doubt, the best guides to the future, but the Titan taught men other signs also by which to make a pretty fair guess at what was likely to happen: such as the difference between false dreams and true, the meaning of haunting sounds at night or dawn, and of the flight and habits of birds. He taught them too the more difficult art of calculating probabilities by the shape and colour of the insides of sacrificed animals, and by the general appearance of a sirloin at dinner. By such means he saved many mighty armies, giving the enemy over to destruction instead. Further, he told men what herbs to drink or chew in sickness—a matter in which dogs had some knowledge, but man none—whether helibore was best, or mandragora, or mint, or poppy-seed, or fox-glove, or garlic which

THE FIRE OF PROMETHEUS 113

gives heroic heart; and what was good as a soothing plaster for wounds, whether pounded nipple-wort or grated cheese mingled with honey. Then he taught them the use of the wheel, and how saving it was to harness other animals than themselves to their carts. More wonderful still, he made the white-winged wagons that flit across the sea. In crystal he showed them thin veins of rustless gold, and from lumps of uncouth rock he hammered out the sword.

'One singularly beautiful gift of a very different kind he also gave them, though the poets have not made much of it, perhaps because, having it in abundance themselves, they hardly realised its beauty. You remember how the Titan said:

"I stopped man looking at the truth of fate,
And in his heart I lodged the blinding hopes."

'That is the golden gift which casts a golden gleam about the world, making the sun appear more glorious than he is, and giving deeper blues and blacks and greens to the sea; making the sea, indeed, appear to be a beautiful or terrific being, though we know it is only so many jugsful of salted water, and to a dog or horse it is dangerous and nasty to drink, but no more. For the dog and horse see the truth of fate; they see the bare facts of things, and when they come to a stream they drink of it, but do not worship. Man alone is blinded by the Promethean gift, and passing over reality with indifference, he fixes his vision on things which are not there. In the translucent pools of the stream he alone can see the beautiful spirit sitting with amber hair, just as the lover beholds something beatified and divine in his maiden, who very likely is only a poor unwashed and witless thing, not in the least nobler than himself. In his own heart also man is blinded to grim fate, and sees a finer spirit than exists. No one appears to himself quite so bad as he really is. When he had to die, the matricide lamented what an artist was dying, and in his own judgment Phalaris would have deserved the hemlock almost as little as the Philosopher. Wherever he moves through the world, man sees around him the fool, the knave, the scoundrel, the murderer, the swindler, the luster, the drunkard, the glutton, the coward, the traitor, the hypocrite, the braggart, the idiot, the gossip, the weakling, the mean and crawling soul. Yet in mankind, which is a combination of all these indifferent creatures, he sees something great and admirable; in the midst of unnatural cruelty he speaks of humanity as though it were the common possession of the human race, and of virtue as the proper quality of man. Some indeed are so richly endowed with these blinding and beneficent hopes, that they move through the world as though they had but one step to reach the

Blessed Isles, of which they see the assurance in the colours of sunset clouds, or in the riding moon, or in the gleams of loveliness that flit across men's hearts like sunshine on dark mountains. By such men evil things are speedily forgotten, and a radiance of joy dances before their eyes. To them the common scenes of earth are illuminated by a glamour of sweet or heroic associations, and even through the ceilings of domestic architecture they ever behold the stars. Sad and impatient they may well be, overcome by a wild yearning for something which even their hearts can hardly imagine, yet they are surrounded by a glory which exists but for them, and is nowhere found. Or may we perhaps say that in a sense it actually exists by their means, and that their passionate conception has indeed the power to create the things they seek; just as lovers create something that is themselves and yet separate and substantial?

Or if that thought appears to you too beautiful even for hope, let us remember what the Iberians say; for they dwell upon the verge of Ocean, and ever watching westward for the Blessed Isles with illimitable desire, about once every seven years they actually behold those islands far away, quivering with beauty on the horizon's rim. And thereupon they all set out in coracles, canoes, and boats of hide, with fire in their hearts and hands, for they know very well that if they can once fling fire on that enchanted land, it will abide with them for ever and be their home. Ah, son of mine,' he went on, stroking the dead man's head, 'on what land of desire did you seek to fling the fire of your soul? And what haven is this that you have found?'

As he seemed lost in thought, I said: 'There it is again. You speak of the fire of the soul; but I only know that Prometheus brought fire to man in a fennel-stalk, and when you said that in this poor fellow here the fire of Prometheus had gone out, you were not speaking of the same fire as the kitchen grate, I suppose, excellent and comforting as that is.'

He smiled shyly and rubbed his hairy face between his hands, on which the blood lay black.

'How you drive me on,' he said, 'worse than the gadfly! Did we not agree that the outer and inner fires were probably of the same nature, their manifestations being so closely alike?'

'Oh, if you are going to talk in symbols,' I said, 'it is hopeless for an ordinary man like me.'

'And yet,' he answered, 'you yourself are but a symbol of the fighting soul upon her perilous way. Well, I can only repeat the things I myself heard long ago and in a different place to this.

'It was late twilight when I crept down the mountain cliffs to where the

Titan lay. For in the daytime many strange beings came to see him—not only the tender mermaids, but that poor cow-headed thing, and Ocean with a shopman's reverence for success and his suspicion of people who have come down in the world. So I waited till his other visitors had gone, and then I crept along the edge to where he lay, indistinguishable from rock, save for the heaving of his breath. I stood beside him in silence, for there was nothing to say, and I saw his great limbs, how wearily they hung, being tortured and clamped with spikes and metal bands. But as midnight passed, and I watched Orion and the Pleiades and all the chilly stars going on their way without a sign of care, I touched his arm where it was pinned to the rock, and said: "Son of Earth, I too am here." But he made no more answer than the rock. Then I lay down beside him, warding off the frost with my nice furry skin, and all night long he hung there silent. But when first a glimmer of white stole into the eastern sky, I spoke again: "Son of Earth, I too am here, for a flame consumes me." And at the word he moved, as the rock of Caucasus stirs beside the streams of ice. Then a voice came, low and proud: "It was I brought flame to man, when before he was colder than dumb fishes."

'Again he was silent, and as the white dawn slowly grew, I said: "Son of Earth, a flame consumes me, seeing what injustice a god suffers at the hands of gods."

'Then he answered: "It was I brought flame to man, the flame for his hearth and his frozen hands. And as I bore it swiftly to earth the sparks kept streaming behind me like a comet's hair, and they mingled with the shivering spirits of unborn men. Into their very hearts the fire entered, and was made one with their blood. There it smoulders for ever, and at a breath it kindles, nor can it ever be quenched, for it is passed on from life to life. In the soul of the men I loved, the fire is kindled which shall avenge me. At the blast of its fury the gods themselves shall wither, and long ages after they have shrivelled like beaten lead in the melting-pot, the fire of my gift shall glow and quicken in the heart of man, nor shall Ocean himself avail to quench it. They into whose blood one spark of it has entered shall never rest from their defiance. Titans of mankind, pity and wrath shall not suffer them to be at peace. At the breath of injustice they shall blaze into fury, so that before them the proclamations of heaven and earth shall shrink into nothingness, and statutes of stone be burnt like withered leaves. All the wealth and power of the world shall ally themselves with the thunders of the gods to tread them down, but defeated in every battle they shall never doubt of victory, for the conflict is their reward, and in the blood of their suffering they shall win their desire. Lean and disquiet they shall be, and nothing shall tempt them from their wrath. No paradise of delight shall give them comfort, nor can their indignation be appeased by all the promises of heaven. Pinned and clamped immovably to the rocks of fate, scorched by derision, frozen by the indifferent stars, torn at heart by the winged ministers of power, they shall not temper their defiance, though the world were one chrysolite, to be theirs in exchange. For these are they who dare to be sad, and have the courage to mate with sorrow. Unobserved they shall toil in the fields or pass up and down the streets of cities, but their souls are wild as the desert where lions tread it only. Therefore let the gods send all the aviary of heaven to devour my heart, let them split my flesh with spikes of steel, or spurn me down the crags of the abyss to roll with earthquakes in the furnaces of hell—wherever that little spark shall glimmer in man's soul, there my avenger goes. O children of men, on whom I had pity, I charge you never suffer the flame of my indignation to die! In your soul from age to age it shall kindle, it shall work. When most it seems to sleep, it shall but gather rage to blaze anew, giving you no peace till the fury of its wrath is satisfied, and consuming with its flickering tongue the fortresses where injustice like the injustice of the gods had thought to dwell everlastingly at ease behind its battlements."

'So he spoke, and the sun's edge shot above the line of the sea, for day had come and the gods were at ease in heaven. Then I departed to tend my goats, and as I went I heard upon the air the rustling of terrible feathers, and a shadow of wings swooped over the reddening ground. That day my flocks went wandering far, for I paid them little heed, so hot a fire burned in my own heart, as though kindled by the breath of the son of Earth. From that time on how often it has blazed anew, driving me into the very trough of war, one of the queerest places for a shepherd! For though I am but an old god from the country, awe-struck and speechless before the glitter and threatening attitude of all military men, yet I have taken some part, as you know, in many battles, as on that far-off day when I walked up and down the front at Marathon cleaving skulls with a ploughshare, so that the fatted ranks of wealth and slavery shivered before my rustic battle-axe.'

He was silent for a time, and I could see his eyes gleaming with splendid memories. For now the filmy moon had crossed the top of heaven, and faced us from the west.

'Forgive the neighing of an old war-horse,' he said, with a sudden smile.

'Every one forgives that, and really it seems so long ago I can scarcely believe I am the same god. But it is still longer since the rage of the Titans was sent sprawling over the world, and the son of Earth was nailed to his cliff; and yet I suppose something less than two hundred pairs of lovers have sufficed to hand on life from that time down to you. Or even if the right number were four hundred, that would not be very many—not nearly half as many as the men lying dead on this hill to-night— and is it not pleasant to think of all the lovers dear who have been happy in conveying to you so charming a gift as life? To this poor peasant here it was conveyed in like manner, though by a more numerous succession, for the generations of the poor are short. And with his blood they handed on that spark of Promethean fire, imparted with greater similitude than life itself. In the hearts of his creators it smouldered and glowed, till at last the flame was fanned and sped him on so that here he lies, blasted as by the thunderbolt of Zeus.'

'Dear son,' he said, pushing his fingers through the dead man's hair, 'like me you loved the light and rain and the sheep upon the hills. You loved the ploughing ox and the ripening vines. You were happy eating and drinking, and one woman at least liked to have you near her. What was it so filled your soul with rage, that you counted all those things as nothing in the balance? Suddenly the fire grew hot, its smoke stifled your utterance, it gleamed in flame. To your fury it would have been a light task to have stormed the gates of heaven, so wild a blaze streamed along your blood. No gifts, no terms, no promises could twist you from your purpose; you could but kill or die. Nothing but death could hold you quiet, and now you are quiet indeed. Wonder fills me as I behold you, of so great a passion was this small body the shrine. Consecrated by flame, your life was as the life of gods, and by the sacrificial fire of its indignation it has been consumed. See, then, in place of the purple robes of sepulchre, I button up your tattered shirt, and draw your sodden trousers straight. For the cærulean fillets of death, I lay your weathered and sweated cap upon your brows. For the winged sandals of Hermes, conductor of souls, I tie the laces of your heavy boots around your naked feet. And for the fee of death's river, upon your mouth I lay the kiss of reverence and awe.'

The light of another day was now beginning to steal through the mist. Hungry and worn out, I lay back upon the stones, indifferent to whatever might befall, and I heard no more till there came a scraping of nailed boots upon rock and a murmur of low voices. Presently some one kicked me in the side, and cried out:

'Blest if he isn't one of us, and alive, too! And we were just going to bury him. I say, you there! What are you doing, nursing a dead enemy?'

'Oh, he's an enemy, is he?' I said, getting up; 'I had quite forgotten there was such a thing.'

'He's gone clean off his head,' said another. 'Lend a hand to heave the body down.' I took the peasant's arm, and three of the burying party held his other limbs, turning him over so that he might be the easier to carry. Then with a cry all together, we raised him up and bore him down the hill to where the dead were laid out in a row. His head nodded, face downwards, between his shoulders.

'Lift up a bit, or you'll knock him against the rocks,' I said to the man who held the other arm.

'That won't do him much damage,' was the reply, 'but up he comes!'

IV

VERTICORDIA

The months go by, and yet it is not so very long since, with an unaccustomed sense of social and spiritual distinction, I enjoyed the respected position of guest in the Deanery of a cathedral town. I had lately returned from a disastrous war in an eastern land, and perhaps on that account it was all the more refreshing that from my bedroom's open casement in the morning, like some cloistered monk, I could watch the sunlight and shadow moving over the grey cathedral's peaks and precipices, or hear the chanted Amens of the early service sounding across the faultless grass, as they had sounded for centuries of innocent and quiet life. Like some pilgrim on his progress, I had passed from life on campaign to an abode where involuntary hunger was undreamt of, where violent death was unknown, and earthly nature was distilled to the purity of dew. There one could rise to heights of almost patristic meditation, whether brooding among the grave bookshelves of the Dean's library, or walking tiptoe down the sanctuary's aisles, half afraid of breaking the tranquillity of a chastened and indwelling spirit. Vergers, canons, and sometimes the very Bishop himself, stole silently about, with faces of unspotted but amiable rigour, far aloof from the world. Even the errand-boys wore a subdued and ethereal look, caught from the choristers, and the gardeners were catholic and apostolic in their demeanour. What it was that gave so peculiar a sweetness to the sound of maidservants' voices rising from the kitchen or the hall, I could hardly say. It may have been the contrast—the delicate harmony in contrast—of their presence in a place so permeated with the spiritual life; or perhaps it was merely that delight in a woman's voice which all men know when wars are done.

On my third evening, I was returning with one of the Canons from a tea-party which the Bishop gave every month to the most select tradespeople of the city, in the belief that episcopalian hospitality mitigated the acrimony of Dissent. It had been a day which to many would have seemed pure and quiet as the Liturgy. The ancient buildings slumbered in holy calm, and within the high-walled garden gentility sat brooding like the dove. But from hour to hour I had felt that the sky and living earth were all astir with suppressed emotion. The air had been purified by rain and wind; and now and again some ragged little cloud came dancing up from the distant sea. Under the chestnut trees I could hear the leaves unfolding their sticky buds. The woods were full of multitudinous little noises, and along the hedgerows birds twittered and fluttered with the shy excitement of children who possess a secret they could tell. For Spring was coming slowly, but it was certain now, and all the ground sent up the faint and delicate smell of it.

As we left the palace the sun was almost down. Here and there a rook steered homeward through the blue, and above the sunset the slender moon hung quivering with expectation. I do not know whether it was that the winning purity of the air produced within the Canon a certain recrudescence of youth, or whether he was slightly elated by taking tea with the Bishop's wife. At all events he began talking theology, and I observed upon his refined and clear-cut face an illuminated look as though another man were peering through it— the man that in his heart he always was, or thought he might easily become at any moment. That is the man he was

(I thought to myself) when as an undergraduate he solved the problems of the universe upon the Cumnor hills; and I remember that as we passed under the old gateway into the Close itself, and our footsteps crunched upon the trim gravel path beside the row of elms, he was speaking of the conversion of St. Augustine—how his heart was changed, and like a man transformed he turned away from the pleasures and other necessary evils of the world. I listened as intently as I could, for theology, like medicine, is of universal interest; but full in front of us rose the grey cliff of the cathedral, and in the midst of his words I could not help perceiving with joy that, like grey Hymettus, even its holy stones were flushed with crimson beneath the touch of the evening radiance.

The Canon, perhaps noticing my sudden inattention, laid his hand gently on my shoulder; for he had reached that stage of clerical and celibate affectionateness.

'My friend,' he said, 'you hang too much on the things of this world. You are still like St. Augustine in his youth, engrossed in its interests, its beauty, and its pleasures.'

'Is it not a vale of tears?' I answered.

'By reason only of its error,' he quickly interposed,—'its error and the unfathomable abyss of human sin. The grossness of man is the one monstrous and incredible phenomenon in a universe otherwise so fair. His sin alone stands like something distorted, unproportioned, and incommensurable within the fair scheme of things. How seldom does he rise above the level of the beasts! With all his indefinable spiritual powers, with his capacity for redemption and the apprehension of ineffable truth, he none the less abides wallowing with them in the sensual sty. People talk a great deal nowadays about man's poverty, his sorrow, and his pain. Many deplore his limited life, his limited capacity for joy.

Such things are but trifles compared to his sin. For sin his capacity is infinite; and do you suppose you would reduce it if you made his outward surroundings as lovely and delicate as this Close?'

'I don't know,' I answered, 'but it would be an easier experiment to make the Close as unlovely and indelicate as man's common surroundings, and watch the effect upon the conduct of its inmates.'

'I confess,' he continued, not noticing my suggestion, 'the vision of the sin diffused in the outer world must often appal us. Our soul shrinks from it as from physical contamination, and we seem to have no more strength left to face the pervading horror of man in his indistinguishable degradation. Then it is that with our utmost power we turn our contemplation upon the Church for our solace and refreshment. There she still remains, unspotted and unmoved— not, we trust, entirely separated from the world, but like our dear cathedral rising high above the common earth on which she stands. Beyond the welter of man's grossness and perversity she soars, ever suggesting an infinity of spiritual development. By the strictness of her ordinances she strives to purify the soul. As with spire and pinnacle and pointed arch, she directs the eyes upward. By the beauty of her services and holy places, by the comeliness of her sacrificial raiment, she attracts, she guides, and disciplines the erring heart, turning the desire from the garish joys of earth towards the glory which she alone has power to reveal. By the persistence and regularity of her ritual, even by its very monotony, she inculcates a habit of holiness, undeviating from its chastened path, till at length the struggle with the brutish elements of our nature results in their extinction. Thus she abides, the sole light in a darkened world, and outside the circle

VERTICORDIA

of her rays, what spiritual hope is left upon man's horizon?'

'I understand your metaphor,' I answered, 'for love has also been described, apparently without irony, as an ever-fixed mark, that looks on tempests and is never shaken.'

'For myself,' the Canon continued, 'I should prefer for the Church the old similitude of the sheep-fold, in which we are ordained as shepherds. Outside stretches the wilderness of the world, howling with empty winds and ravening desires. But within the fold we still keep our little flock untouched and pure from the surrounding evil, just as this Close, encircling our holy edifice, is preserved by us from the uncouth monsters of human grossness, from the vulgarities of passion, and whatever else may offend, so that within our sacred precincts all may be purity and peace for ever.'

He paused, with eyes fixed in contemplation of so fair a vision, and a terror seized me that he was departing from the equal ground of man and man. Chilled and panic-stricken, I looked around for refuge, like the poor dosser whose untutored mind espies a philanthropist in the offing. We were close to the cathedral's western doors, and with a sense of relief I perceived that from every corner and lurking-place in the porches, strange creatures of stone thrust out their peering heads or seemed to shrink and hide. Uncouth monsters certainly they seemed, and their ambiguous forms trailed in dragon folds along the mouldings, where their semi-human bodies ended in the feet of goats. But on the face of all was the look of men and women, and from their empty sockets came the yearning of exiled or imprisoned souls.

But by the Canon all those comforting gargoyles were unheeded. Even St. Augustine was forgot, and in speechless astonishment he was watching a slight feminine figure which hastened along one of the cross-paths over the grass. She wore uniform—the white apron and shoulder-straps of the domestic service corps, and there was still light enough to show a fluff of ruddy hair under the pure white cap.

'*Can* it be? It *must* be. It *is* Elizabeth,' I heard the Canon mutter to himself. And then, in his lectern voice, he cried: 'Elizabeth, is that you?'

The girl stopped short, and began twisting the corner of her apron round her fingers. 'Yes, sir, please sir,' she said. 'I've just been to drop a letter in the post, sir.'

She turned hastily away, and unhappily, in turning, showed the white cross-bands over her shoulders. Between them lay a clear triangle of black dress, and right in the very centre of that triangle was seen the definite impress of a great white hand—palm, thumb, and all the fingers, 'displayed,' as the heralds say. There was no mistaking it. Even a man of peace could not fail to recognise the pipe-clay brand of the British army.

'Then shall the lion lie down with the lamb, and within our sacred precincts all shall be purity and peace for ever,' I murmured to myself, recalling the Canon's vision of beatitude.

I hoped the tell-tale mark had escaped his notice, but I was wrong.

'Elizabeth,' he called after her in a deeper tone.

'Yes, sir,' she said, turning to us again, so that the symbol of glory disappeared.

'I think you have something white on the back of your dress.'

'No, sir, I've not, sir,' she said, and instantly her hand sought the exact place between her shoulders, and tried in vain to brush it.

'To me,' continued the Canon with real solemnity, 'to me it suggests the figure of a man's hand.'

The girl looked this way and that, and then gave up. Throwing her apron over her face in token of surrender, she cried from behind that feminine defence: 'O sir, you do not know how sweet it is!'

No appeal could have been more eloquent, and I looked to see the Canon falter, but he showed no more hesitation than the Athanasian Creed. 'Elizabeth,' he said, 'I desire you to re-enter the house immediately and pack your box.'

Without a word the girl hurried away, and fixing his eyes on the gravel, the Canon said to himself: 'The cook will see it; Mary will see it. It will revive their natural propensities. This is terrible, most terrible.'

'And yet,' said a low voice close at hand, 'fire is the best sauce. Evenus said so.'

In the twilight under the elms I beheld a weather-worn figure. His eyes were following the girl with the regretful look of one who has lost an opportunity.

'You see, sir,' he said, turning to the Canon, 'I am but a humble shepherd, and now you have driven away my flock, so that I fear lest I should lose it—a bitter thing for shepherds, as you know. For as you approached I overheard you saying that you also were a shepherd, and kept the silly sheep in fold.'

'I meant a shepherd of souls,' said the Canon absently.

'Of souls, no doubt,' the other replied, 'but not, I suppose, of disembodied souls, any more than I, though but a common shepherd, tend the soulless bodies of dead sheep. Unless, perhaps, with your crook you catch the soul escaping from the body's prison, as the pastoral poet describes it in his verse on sheep-shearing:—

> "The shepherd sits like death who takes his toll;
> The struggling sheep secure before him lies,
> And feels the encumb'ring fleeces off her roll,
> And, naked, stands at gaze with dubious eyes;
> Then rushes forth, like a bewildered soul,
> Escaping, cool and white, to Paradise."

Souls may, indeed, escape by some such queer process, but I can hardly suppose your care extends to them after they are stript of the body's fleece?'

'Elizabeth in the arms of a common soldier!' groaned the Canon. 'And it is hardly six months since I myself prepared her for confirmation.'

'Nay, sir,' said the shepherd soothingly, 'I did not know that you also had a claim on her, for I thought she was in my sole charge to-night. But since it is so, could we not come to some arrangement about the matter? Let us, for example, contend in amœbæic song, as shepherds use, and set the lamb to be the winner's prize. Or perhaps you would prefer the rivalry of the oaten pipe?'

The vision of himself playing a panpipe in the Close was too much for the Canon's dignity. Turning to the shepherd for the first time, he exclaimed with some irritation, in spite of his general politeness: 'Really, my good fellow, I must remind you that in this Close no one except the Dean is allowed to walk upon the grass.'

'It is quite like old times to hear of the worship of grass,' said the shepherd; 'and, indeed, grass like this is a holy thing for weanling lambs to eat. Let us, therefore, recline rather upon this bench for our contest. The evening wind is warm, and the white-limbed moon is stealing to her lover behind the woods; Hesper hangs low from the depth of air, and the lambs are folded beneath the open sky. Begin with me, dear sir, the strain of Mænalus. Or, if you will not begin, let my turn come the first.

'Far away in Arcadia, overshadowing the Tegean plain, where the children of black earth turn their mother-soil, Mount Mænalus yet stands, and his head looks northward to snowy Cyllene, where Aphrodite dwelt. His precipitous sides are wet with melting snows; they gleam in the fitful sunlight. The soft rain falls; green are the slopes of his pastures, and there the she-goat leads her young. Year by year the spring has passed over his crest from the times of old when gods danced there. The seasons go, the gods are gone, but he is ever new, and sure as hope and love. He himself shall vanish from the world, but hope and love remain. Now is the season of love and hope, when all things are renewed. All things are new, but none so new as is the lover's heart. The tender leaf is like last year's leaf; and last year the snow ran down in streams like this. But love is newer than the morning, and the lover's heart to-day is such a thing as never was before. Begin with me, dear sir, Mænalian strains.'

'That sort of stuff is all very pretty,' said the Canon, 'but for my part I reserve the word love for holier things. I agree with the man in the play who said: " Let us determine to call a mere sensual instinct by as few fine names as possible."'

'I implore you,' answered the shepherd, 'not to summon the poet's aid in putting the gods to open shame. It is sad to find how far you stand behind the Egyptians in consideration for them. For you remember that in Egypt all worshippers knew as a fact that the gods had once been men, but decency forbade them to say so. In the same way, none but the ungentle and impious should throw up his humble descent against love. It is quite true that, like man's own, his origin was distinctly low. For he was born in the green twilight of the warm primæval sea, before the surface fires of earth were cold. When first the lumps of living jelly drifted over the shallows of heaving slime, love was already there. Among the crawling dragons of the swamp he had his home, and where the ravening monsters cried, he made his habitation. Poor hairy creatures were glad at his coming, and he was foster-brother to the wolf. Even then he possessed a power which I can hardly describe, for it was unlike all the other powers of men and gods. You remember what the poet says of love's mother, as she went through the forests of Ida, where wild beasts find their food:

> "She through the mountain coverts took her way,
> And close behind her tender footsteps came
> Devouring leopard things, and wolves all grey,
> Wild bears, and lions staring fixèd flame,
> Which she beholding was fulfill'd with cheer,
> And in their desert hearts she set her longings dear."

In those lines is it not reasonable to suppose that unless the old poet had perceived, even in his day, something marvellous and inscrutable in the power of love, he would have spoken of gentle antelopes and doves rather than of bears and lions grim? But if love's longing can indeed produce so comfortable a change even in uncouth and savage beasts, let us no longer mock at his homely origin, rejoicing rather that, no matter from what source he sprang, so improving a god has been brought into the world of mankind. For we should have been sad enough without him, if what another poet says be true:

> " Without thee, on the holy shore of light
> No living thing appears, nor any joy
> Is found therein, nor lovesomeness at all." '

'It seems to me,' said the Canon, 'that people who believe we are derived from lobsters might just as well sing the praises of a sea-water life, as this so-called love. After all, it is but a sensuous infatuation, and what do the passions of ascidians matter to me, or the passions of swine either?'

'Nothing, certainly, to you,' said the shepherd; 'I only wished to say that upon simple men, as upon the beasts, the god exercises the same peculiar power of change. For it is well known that he makes the coward brave, and the churl almost agreeable; and in the higher ranks of life many a shrinking and fastidious gentleman has been converted at his touch into a bold, bad poet. Therefore it appears to me best not to thwart such powers as his, but, as the Greeks used to say, to let the water run under the bridge. It pities me to think what woe you may have wrought by driving apart my humble sheep to-night. To their souls (you will grant them souls) a supreme moment had arrived. They too were transfigured like the lions and the bears. Full of gentleness and yearning, their hearts transcended the limits of mortality. Companionless no more in space, they beheld the ancient universe transfused with new illumination, and had no fear of all the world. On returning to barracks, the soldier would have answered his name as though it were a duke's title. In waiting at your table to-night, your serving-maid would have moved an equal to the youthful ministrant of gods, and had she dashed your pottery to the ground, she would have felt no qualm, recognising wealth for the dust it is, compared to love. But now perchance they are parted for ever, and their souls will wander in desert places, crying in vain. It may be that even yet, though Hesperus has followed sun and moon into the sea-sepulchre of renovation, it were best for me to seek them out and bring them to each other's sight. For, in truth, lovers are only safe together.'

'Unsafe, you mean,' interposed the Canon, ' and if you go ringing for Elizabeth at my back-door, I'm afraid I must tell the cook not to admit you.'

'To be turned from the door is the destiny of low estate,' said the shepherd. 'That is the worst of being only a layman in the gods' service.'

'Fine gods, indeed!' said the Canon, with his politest smile.

'Common rather than fine,' answered the shepherd, 'for this evening I was in the service of Mars and Venus, both quite ordinary deities, connected from of old by an illicit understanding. Indeed, at this time of year, as you know, all shepherds like me serve Venus among their flocks, and it is impossible, I suppose, to serve the beloved without serving the lover too; since their hearts are always one.'

'Better among sheep than with a soldier and a housemaid!' cried the Canon. 'Common is certainly the word for your deities of unrestraint and vulgar abandonment!'

'You must excuse me, sir,' said the shepherd, 'for even mentioning a theme so humble. You see, it is easy for the rich and intellectual to gain the peace of the gods. They do it every day, and still have plenty of time over to condemn the ignorance, imprudence, and vices of the poor. But for my own charges, I am full of anxiety lest in the scurry of their hunger and toil they should miss any of their skimpy opportunities of grace in the few brief hours before they are wiped away, like the sums upon a child's slate —washed out, may we not think? by the tears of their distracted creator, because they will not come right.'

'When a domestic servant acquiesces in the animal instincts of a soldier,' said the Canon, 'I admire your courage in speaking of opportunities of grace. Disgrace is likely to prove the more suitable word.'

'That may be so,' replied the shepherd with unruffled calm; 'but still I discern an opportunity for—what shall I say? Will you allow me to use the word transfiguration?'

'The transfiguration from my house to the haunts of sin is certainly considerable,' cried the Canon impatiently. 'And not to understand what it implies shows ignorance of the world and of common sense.'

'I was thinking rather of an inner and spiritual change,' said the shepherd. 'But as to my ignorance you are certainly right. For who can know the world's depth and height? And for common sense, even the gods have seldom shown it.'

Seeing that the Canon was slightly irritated at the poor man's simplicity, and not wishing to witness a contest between two such shepherds within the Close itself, I hastily tried to divert the dialogue towards some wider theme. 'That word transfiguration has a very solemn sound,' I said; 'but I suppose that in spite of its solemnity there is some sort of meaning in it?'

'I half think so,' said the shepherd, with a puzzled look. 'It is hard to say exactly what it is—hard, I mean, for me; though whatever the explanation may be, I have heard lovers say that the change is true. But I knew how it would be if I dared to approach so near to wisdom and use magnificent words. For such teaching I had far better commend you to the smile of golden Venus herself when she fingers her loosened zone. One of her many names, you know, is Verticordia; I suppose because she transfigures the heart.'

'For centuries the Church struggled against the foulness of her degradation,' said the Canon; 'and are we to turn to her now as a transfiguring power?'

'Many evil things, indeed, have been said of her,' the shepherd went on; 'but a few nice things too. There is a pretty Greek sentence, that love in a gloomy man is like a cheerful fire in a cold house; and you know what a difference that makes. The Argives used to say that the soul of a lover resided in the soul of the beloved, and they were not people to philander over the affections like writers of flim-flam tales. If then the soul can really quit her home and dwell in the beloved's life, is not that a transfiguration enough? And may we not say that the soul in her flitting then changes self as well as sky? Moreover,

I have heard physicians say, the physical senses of lovers are redoubled, so that they become quick as the senses of woodland creatures, and across the desert of a public assembly, lovers will hold intercourse with their eyes, enough to populate all fairyland. For they understand the words of silence, and at the thought of the beloved's voice, or at the faint sound of it, coming upon them suddenly from far off, their hearts stop beating, and they stand quivering with rapture. If, then, the lover's senses, which are the feeders and instruments of the soul, are thus intensified to new powers, may we not suppose that the soul herself is transfigured, at least to a like degree?'

'But even you,' I answered, 'would hardly maintain that Venus is the only transfiguring power.'

'I am not quite sure,' said the shepherd. 'A similar change is certainly seen in the service of love's lover and opposite—the crimson plague of men, who batters cities down. We need not speak of his influence on kings and generals, such as history disembowels and embalms. But you at all events have witnessed the change in humble craftsmen and tillers of earth who form the fighting ranks. Their life is short, to each of them it is very dear, and they long to enjoy it to the full. Some delight in laughter and wine; some follow prudence, who is the grandmother of the little virtues, and at times rewards them with an approving sixpence. Some love their children, some their parents or friends, some their comforts, others their possessions; all love women. Yet, with a light heart, they endure discomforts in war time which at home would have exposed their wives to continuous blasphemy, and as though to win the best places at a lascivious show, each rushes forward in furious emulation to climb the ruin of the breach and be the first to enter the hostile city as a corpse.

Is it not strange, is it not a marvel that so diverse a soul should dwell within one man? Who would have suspected these hidden qualities in a sane and mortal creature? Compared to the marvel of the soul's change under a god's inspiration, there is no miracle ever performed in earth or heaven which I would turn my head to see or wag my little finger to accomplish.'

'Blithe shepherd,' I said hastily, for fear the Canon should take offence again, what you say about war reminds me of the proverb that love is an invincible general, and in my boyhood I remember reading of some leader who composed a battalion entirely of loving comrades, setting them two by two together in the ranks, so that they became incapable of defeat; for even though separated on the field, a man would hold his ground as long as he thought his comrade was fighting on. And I have somewhere read the lines:—

"Backwards and forwards, up and down the land,
　　The battle rolls unending, and the air
Thickens with mist of blood and columned sand,
　　Hiding the souls in lingering conflict there.

My comrade, it was morning when we parted,
　　'Tis evening now, the foe is on the flanks;
My comrade, here I stand unshaken-hearted,
　　Knowing that somewhere you are in the ranks."

That is the comradeship of war, and do you not think, that if Mars and his lover could indeed combine their inspiration on the battlefield, we might acquire an army of unexampled valour? For, kindled by god and goddess alike, and terrified lest the beloved at his side should suffer by one hair's loss, the lover would fling himself upon the enemy with irresistible passion, and in his vengeance be more terrible than a regiment of uninspired men.'

'It is a very charming brigade which you imagine,' replied the shepherd: 'all the men in the front rank and their lovers behind them. Their bivouacs beneath the moon on summer nights

vould be especially delightful. My fear
s that in battle, instead of advancing
ver forward, the lover would only stand
s shelter for the beloved, lest wounds
efall her beauty, and slit her lovesome
kin. In case of sudden alarm, it is
rue, such an army would have great
dvantage at first, for each man would
pring to his place with his lover behind
im, and no time would be lost in
umbering or telling off. But I have
eard say that love hath wings and lovers
lange, and might not confusion arise
 two or three in either the front or
ar rank had fixed their affections upon
 new object only a few minutes before
le alarm was sounded? It is unlikely
at they should be able simply to change
aces among themselves, and if the new
ver found his desired position in file
ready occupied, disorder would arise,
d the ranks would fall to internal
ife, endangering victory. For desire
 be near the beloved is more powerful

even than the fear of defeat and death. Do you not think so?'

'I hardly know what to think,' I replied, 'for you have extended my simple conceit into a similitude of the wide world, in which men and women arrange their files as though they were eternally lovers, but afterwards pine for disturbing changes.'

'There,' said the Canon, with a smile of triumph, 'there lies the irremediable weakness of this earthly passion; there the falsity of all the fine things sung in its praise. It is animal, therefore temporal. It is for us to fix our thoughts on the things that are eternal.'

'Ah, well,' said the shepherd, 'I suppose we must not be too exacting with the gods. Life is a stream, and nought abides. Even the stars stare themselves blind and die. We must love them whilst they shine, and trust that future stars will gleam no less. We eat to-day, though to-morrow we may starve. A lover looking back on past love reminds me of Pythagoras when, in a temple at Argos, he found the armour which in a previous existence he had himself worn during the siege of Troy. Perhaps his former body also lay under it, yet he raised no idle lamentation over that ancient skeleton, but was only thankful he had another set both of armour and of bones to bless himself with. Tragic indeed the disarrangements you speak of may sometimes appear, especially in the case of the best soldiers in your delightful army; and it is only the tragedy of the best that counts. Yet even in the midst of their unhappy perturbations we can perceive the light of the god's transfiguring power, and at times I can even imagine an abiding influence, which might almost be called eternal without absurdity—as eternal as the gods themselves, I mean; though, to be sure, that is not saying much. So now, having worshipped love by extolling his might among wild beasts and simple men, we may as well depart, especially as it is near the hour for us who obey the kindly influence of heaven, to submit ourselves to the night and stars like mountain goats.'

'Gentle shepherd,' I said, 'may I say that you remind me of a nightingale, almost as much as of a goat?'

'Oh, if you are going to begin upon riddles,' cried the Canon, getting up, 'I will go and see what chance we have of dinner to-night. Our friend tells me that if her love had run smooth, Elizabeth would have dashed my china to the ground without a qualm; and now that the affair is happily detected, *a fortiori*, she may be doing worse. I only hope I shall not find the soldier sitting among the ruins of my pantry.'

'A soldier is a terrible thing for kitchens, like the wolf for sheepfolds,' said the shepherd.

'A transfigured soldier is a sheep in wolf's clothing,' said the Canon.

He went off, smiling to himself at having the last word; and drawing nearer to the shepherd on the ecclesiastic bench, I continued:

'You know the nightingale, how when spring is young, he utters but a few notes, and those harsh and out of tune, and then he falls to silence with a kind of despairing gasp, as though he would say, "It is no good; I shall never sing like the blackbird or the thrush!" And so he goes on, evening after evening, perhaps unconscious of his power, perhaps dissimulating with modest irony, until one night when all the woods are still, some lover, watching the candle in his beloved's bedroom, perchance may hear a longdrawn cry of exquisite and unutterable yearning, and will say to himself, "That is the nightingale! Ah, if only his voice were mine!" But for a fortnight more the brown little bird will twitter again, nursing in secret all the passion of his life, and only rising at the very last to his full rapture of unconstrained delight, as though to reveal to the whole listening world what singing really is. So if indeed it is the same with you—if you are keeping back some magic word or secret song or hidden knowledge—I entreat you of your courtesy to let me hear it now. It may be that for the last time I hear you speak. Year slides after year; war is really rather dangerous, and nothing is so dangerous as life. So speak now, that I may not go out into the dark uncomforted.'

He looked at me as though with sad affection, but immediately recovering his accustomed cheerfulness, he turned away and began laughing low to himself.

'Do you not think the priest would mock,' he said, 'if on his return he found two adult persons still discoursing upon love? Under that spiky temple too, whose blackness just blots out the constellation of Andromeda, chained to a sea-rock amid the pitiless benedictions of her relatives, till love delivered her! He would be like an astronomer who, knowing for a fact that the little moon was only the sunlit edge of a lifeless ball of rock, should overhear two benighted pagans joyfully praising that thin curve of brightness as a chaste huntress queen, whose lithe and tender form well matched her crescent bow. And if he further heard them tell how once upon a time, as she sank into the woods to hide among her forest things, the woodland god did woo her, and she rejected him not, she who rejected all—why, then, no doubt, the astronomer would laugh, like a suburban resident fallen among country folk.'

'Or, perhaps, if he were a magistrate, he might get them shut up for lunacy,' I said.

'In the same way,' he continued, 'the priest, who evidently knows far more about the scientific nature of love than either of us, would laugh or rage to hear the strange illusions and dreams which simple men have woven around so plain and obvious a matter. Such eremites of the spirit naturally breathe a higher air than ours, and we cannot wonder that this poor old earth looks gross and dusty from their ethereal seats. It is seldom that her voice reaches them up there, and when it does, they listen shuddering, or smile with downcast eyes at the thought of the elevation to which they have been wafted. But we poor children of the sand, who still are gathered close to the breasts of earth, and lie entangled in her hair of grass and forest, marvelling in our childlike simplicity at the sweetness of her voice in winds and sea and living things—we, I suppose, may listen without shame to the strange outcries and imaginations of man among the rest, and perhaps we should not be much distressed if the wise contemn the homely dreams which poor earthly lovers tell us about Verticordia and things of that kind. They are sometimes sweet to hear, and we need not suppose them meaningless because, love being so shy and fugitive a thing, even lovers can hardly get a sight of him except disguised in some veil of dream. Once, it is true, I have heard that he was very nearly seen, disembodied as it were, and without his skin and bones, just as you would like to catch a human soul as it flits away from the beloved's outworn heart. But even you, ignorant and earthly as you are, would hardly listen to such a tale seriously.'

'Yes,' I answered, 'I will be as solemn as a City dinner during the grace.'

He was silent a while, and then continued with much hesitation: 'Once upon a time (for that is the only date which really matters), an ambiguous creature was sitting at the Great Mother's feet and looking up into her face as she mingled the souls and bodies of living things in her kneading-trough. I could see from her eyes that all was not going well, for she had the distressed look of a woman when the bread will not rise. At last, throwing down a lump of the half-living clay in despair, and driving it off in the form of a hippopotamus, whereas she had intended it for a Justice of the Peace, she cried: "Dear dog-of-all-work, I really do not know what has come over the race of man. With my other pleasant creatures I am as successful as ever. That lion, just issuing into the upper light, is as fleet and strong as the royal beasts which Ashur-bani-pal hunted in his chariots with dogs and arrows. Like them he will trot loose-jointed over the desert; like them, with ears thrown back and thin-pinched flank, he will roar his hot heart to the moon; like them he will tenderly lick his yellow-eyed mate among the rocks, and with those terrible paws caress her velvet side. But man is sick and different. I am sure I try my very best to make him as nicely as ever, but for some reason or another he is unsatisfied and unhappy. A sadness has fallen on him, and an evidence of his sickness is that men and women no longer openly delight in being together, with nothing but the cheerful god of love between them, as in the days when you and I were younger than we are. They crawl away into deserts, there to lie groaning and tormenting themselves, as though they could not be wretched enough without deliberately increasing their misery. Surely some curse lies on them, shrivelling and distorting their nature, like a blight in corn. I really cannot think what to do with them. Hitherto man has been a very nice little fellow, but now he is getting beyond me, as the nursemaids say, and if I had my own will I would give up making him, and fashion only savage things. So sick am I at the failure that I will go visit for a while the blameless

Ethiopians, who are still unspoiled and happy, and in my absence I pray you watch the streams of life as they flow. As diversion you can try your hand on a beast or two, if you like, but play no tricks with man. For he looks terribly volcanic, and no one knows what Ætnean monster might arise from his substance now."

'In sadness she departed, bringing joy and plenty to the Ethiopians, and I was left alone in the workshop of life. So, like a schoolboy let loose with a tool-chest, I set to at once, squeezing and moulding the substances into shapes which followed the old models pretty closely. But exact imitation, you know, is impossible, and philosophers tell us that it is individuality which makes the artist. That is why, in my zeal for art, I gave an extra pull to the giraffe's neck; and it was I who bestowed on the flamingo a general's beak, and modelled the adjutant-bird on the portrait of an elderly lawyer. It was I who painted the baboon with vermilion and blue, and gave to the turkey the power of reddening with rage and stiffening out his feathers like a magistrate on the bench. To the sulkiest camels I gave two humps instead of one. I made the elephant's hind-legs bend inwards like a courtier's, and moulded the rhinoceros into a dream of armoured chivalry. Having thus added a pleasing variety to life, I looked out on the world, and saw that all the dear things were delighted with themselves and as happy as the day is long. Blue and red became the national colours of baboons; lady giraffes thought nothing so becoming as a long neck, and the more like a monstrous illusion the rhinoceros looked, the better his mate loved him.

'But when I turned from the gay deserts and the jungles to regard man in places where he boasted himself most like the gods, I perceived the truth of the Great Mother's words. For he kept moving restlessly up and down, as though on some vain search, and what had pleased him before was insufficient now, like toys to a grown youth. Stung by the lash of some power more malignant than the Erinnyes, he hid himself in loneliness, brooding over death and tearing his own flesh because it cried out for satisfaction which no longer satisfied; for I perceived that all the riches of Sardis, all the concubines of Babylon, and the victories of Assyrian kings would now have availed him nothing. The world also was full of cruelty, man rending the life of man in rage at his own indefinable wretchedness; or if in their gloomy cities man and woman met at all, they snatched a haphazard pleasure, in which was no kindly intercourse, or length of affection, or tender solicitude for young ones, or sweet mutual service of food and sleep such as even wild things have, but in ignorance and bitter haste they met and parted. And behind all that is gentle and lovesome upon the variegated crust of earth they espied an ominous peril to their souls, and they scorned the familiar things of mortality, whilst in their eyes smouldered a yearning unappeased for some intangible mystery beyond the confine of this trimly rounded world.

'Full of sorrow at their unhappy state, I had no heart to continue my merry creations, but lay stretched in idleness upon the ground, sad as the wind of memories when now the Eurotas flows under the full Spartan moon and no white feet come dancing to the banks. And as I lay, the streams of life ran past on either hand, lapping against the sides like little waves upon a breakwater. But I let them run unheeded, for it wearied me of life, and being born, as you know, a little old-fashioned, I wept at the thought of man's unhappiness after all the trouble that had been taken with

him. And in sorrow I said to myself,—
"It is time to die now, for they have
again forgotten me, and all my quaint
attributes and darling delights are turned
to fear and derision." Then I stretched
forth my hands on either side, and plung-
ing them into the streams as they ran, I
looked once more upon the stuff which
might have become human, but now was
better uncreated. And lo! under my
touch it began to struggle blindly like
an unborn child, and unwittingly my
hands were drawn closer to each other,
till the substances leapt together with a
cry of joy and were transfused. Terrible
was my perplexity, for I remembered the
Mother's warning, and indeed the stuff
heaving and writhing before me did look
very volcanic. But I yearned over it
with desire for its fulfilment, like a
mother when she feels the baby's shapeless bones begin to stir. Taking it in
my hands, I looked cautiously round,
and saw no one. All was silent but for

the sorrow of the world, which, like the lamentation of reeds, struck in variance across the punctual harmony of the moving stars. Full of that sad sweet sound which is my music, I began to mix and mould the substance, disobeying the greater gods. And as I fashioned the work my tears fell upon it, and were mingled with the half-conscious clay, for into my heart I had gathered up all the long unhappiness of man, and I wept as we primitive things sometimes must. Then I called aloud to love, if perchance he were living still. Once and again I called, but there was no voice that answered. Then I cried to him a third time, for it is at the third call, if ever, that the gods arrive. And waiting with sorrow, I perceived that on a sudden the substance between my hands began to glow with an inner radiance, as though a star of lightning were kindled in its depths. And a voice said, "Love is born again, and into him have passed all the longings and inexhaustible imaginations of mankind."

'Full of astonishment, I caught the radiant substance quickly to my heart, being terrified for its welfare and not knowing what sort of thing this new love might be. But keeping it safe against my hairy breast, I moulded it there into man and woman, gently rending its delicate texture in twain, and with much effort keeping the creatures apart, for they struggled wildly to reunite. And I said to myself: " Being fashioned with my hands and kneaded with my tears, they surely will not forget me. Wherefore should I die?" Then I breathed into their nostrils the breath of the forest and of the mountain pasture and of all seas, and smiling sadly to myself with unanticipated joy, I laid bare their hearts before I closed them up in their breasts, and kissed them as a mother kisses her weanling child the very last time she gives it suck, so that they were filled with laughter which was but half sorrow, and with spendthrift delight and passionate affection intensified by the knowledge of death. Then finishing off their separated flesh as finely as I could, remembering what I had learnt by practice on lions and antelopes, I sent the twain boldly out into the upper air upon their diverse ways.

'So without repining, I returned to my humble labours, having great confidence in the god's power, but from time to time I peered forth to see my dear ones, how they were getting on. Then I perceived that full of hope and an immeasurable passion for something unattained, they roved the earth, and as though by accidents and mistakes were drawn step by step nearer together, whilst the very stars moved with them as in expectation of a god's birth, and the rocks heaved and were troubled, so that, remembering the old prophecy how love should one day bring chaos back again, I shivered at what I had done like a child who lets a tiger loose. And in the midst of creation's travail I heard the angry shrieks of sluggard and sensual souls who were satisfied with common things, and through cowardice dreaded the steps of coming change. Then I looked again and beheld the man and woman standing face to face, aflame with desire for a communion that should transcend the limits of the world, and I saw that the throbbing of the universe did but repeat the throbbing of the lover's heart, for it quivered like a hound in leash, and at the sound of the beloved's salutation it leapt and stood still. As they came near to each other, I perceived also that the radiance of the god who had come in answer to my prayer was again kindled within them, so that the very forms of both were transfused with unearthly light; and when their hearts, being now close together, held converse as though by interwoven music, in which words would hinder rather than help, I knew that in their love was born a strange and incalculable quality—oh, sweeter far than food to the starving or water to the thirsty, or light to those who issue from a mine. For into their spirit was gathered up all the long yearning of mankind for a vision of beatitude beyond the compass of mortality, and of man's glory they found assurance in the unlimited prodigality of their own devotion. Into the service of their love they turned all the old delight of earth, so that the morning sang of it, and the sorrow of its desire lived in the tenderness of the setting sun. It hung upon the horns of the moon, and its voice was heard in the breath of trees and the cadences of the waves. It rose in the smell of the warm ground after rain, and to snow or desert heat it bade an equal welcome. Within their heart also the lovers heard the calling of unimaginable generations to whom aforetime love had given his solace. With their joy of spirit were blended the joys of the far-off and inhuman creatures to whose brief moments of lovingkindness caverns dark and cold gave shelter on shores where the grey sea beat. In their souls the mailed warriors again made love; they knew the happiness of the shepherd returning home, and of the spearman back from war, and they knew the happiness of those who stood to meet them, nor did they feel shame of their love, but only the greater joy, because one single ray of its nature had lightened the eyes of tigers meeting in the night where waters flow.

'And in the music of their diverse harmony I seemed to hear their thoughts speaking in antiphone, as though one said: "Love has no reason but itself"; and the other answered: "It is more blessed to love than to be loved." And one said: "Love can deny nothing to love." And the other answered: "I will not deny even the gift of strange and sweet reserves, that love's lustre be not dimmed." Ever striving for union they rejoiced that, being twain, each might love the other better than the soul loves itself. Seeking for some miracle whereby their spirit might mingle by day and night, they found that the miraculous had already happened. For the first time life was theirs, and for the first time they knew death, how by the foreboding of eternal separation he concentrates the embrace of living flesh into a passion of solicitude hardly to be endured.

'Other words of theirs I might have heard, but I shut my ears, drawing down their furry points, lest even a god should do the lovers wrong through envy and astonishment. For their souls seemed intertwined as the spirit intertwines with the flesh, so that one cannot say, "Here it is," or, "That is it." The air about them was golden with light and quivered like summer heat above a plain, as though it were laden with some unpenetrated secret. The world in their sight was charged with gladness, and to gaze upon that lady the common people ran together, knowing that in her they beheld a miracle. For the lovely joy which radiated from her soul, in touching others became split into various hues like sunshine on a raincloud, so that upon the happy she cast the gold of greater gladness, and on the rebel the green of liberty, and on the mourner the violet of consolation. But upon her lover she threw a scarlet flame, in the midst of which she burned with a light brighter than fire. Thus they entered upon fulness of life, becoming, as the Greeks say, greater than themselves. For they were continually driven to rise above the past, seeing that day by day love had to be conquered afresh, like a persistent enemy, and he refused to surrender himself unto a yesterday's virtue.

'Thus they moved along the track of life with redoubled soul, and like Leto I was full of joy in my miraculous children. For it seemed that with them a new light had risen, far surpassing all that the people of old days had to tell of the brightest affection. And for the rest of mankind, amid the sliding uncertainties of life, it held out a vision of incalculable hope. So the sailors in the wash and swirl of the monotonous but shifting sea, when the wind blowing from Thrace drives the spray along the surface of the black water like fragments of glass—suddenly at midnight they see the white columns of the temple gleaming on the promontory, and the lamps of the priests shining yellow as they move about in service to the god and goddess who rule the sea and air, so that the rude and outcast men take comfort on their way.'

The shepherd was silent for a moment, and I could hardly see him, for the twilight had gone, and clouds were swimming round the earth. 'Such a thing does not often happen,' he went on, laughing as he sighed; 'for that ambiguous creature does not get many chances at the kneading-trough, and think of the myriad passionate souls which are needed to make up one such consummation as a lover's heart! About once in three ages, people say, it may be possible, but a separation of a few years may thwart it —a few miles of water, a few yards of dust or slime or stone. Yet under the similitude of Verticordia, whether she is seen in snails or goats or love's own lovers, lurks one of the powers by which this queer old earth is illumined. If you put your ear to the ground on a spring evening like this, you may hear the mysterious breathing of earth, just as a lover in the stillness of night may lay his head upon the beloved's heart without awaking her, and in its throbbing hear the murmur of the wild and unimaginable generations of warm-beating hearts which have handed down to her the flame of life. As I listen, my marvel grows at the brief but immeasurable glory of my poor human charges. They appear and are gone. Like shipwrecked boys they are cast upon the shoals of time, and drop off into darkness. No research of history, no deciphering of village tombs can ever recover them. We think that somewhere they may still lie nestled up, with all their age about them; but even darkness holds them no more. They stood on this flying earth, we see their footsteps, we hear the thin ghost of their voices, and on the stones lies the touch of their dead hands, but they are nowhere to be found at all. They knew how short their dear life was, yet they filled it with labour and unrecorded toil. Morning and night through their little space of minutes they struggled and agonised to keep on living and feed their children for the struggle and agony of a few minutes more. The sun blasted them, ice devoured their flesh, their mouths were mad with thirst, hunger twisted them with cramps, plague consumed them, they rotted as they stood, bolts of torture drove through their brains, their bodies were clamped into hoops; in battle, in childbed they died with extremity of pain. Yet they endured, and into the chinks and loopholes of their misery they crammed laughter and beauty and a passion transfiguring them beyond the semblance of the gods. My son, let us leave it to the priests to marvel at man's wickedness. At many things I marvel, but over the mere conception of any such thing as love or laughter in the heart of man, I could stand astonished with admiration throughout a god's lifetime.

'It is in vain that, fifty times in succession, man calls himself a miserable sinner. What he ought to recall fifty times in succession is the miracle that it is not true. He knows well enough that, under the flame of passionate devotion, he may find himself fused, moulded, and battered into forms beyond the touch of misery or sin. Below the long drone of uninspired existence, we may still hear the throb of those lifegiving moments when the spirit is transfigured by the virtue of extremes. By those drum-beats life is counted, and nowhere but in extremes does virtue lie. Who has found warmth in the tempered moderation of all the philosophers, or comfort in their reasonable consolations? No misery is so freezing as deliberate happiness; no sin so black as moderated virtue and moderated vice. Who loves a moderate woman, or cares to chase a lion reasonable in his rage? Let us unphilosophic people follow the extremes of the spirit wherever they may lead us, as is the lover's way, hoping to win on our course the lover's reward of uncalculating service. By madness only, or by sleep, it is written, man may enter into the council-chamber of the gods. So now, my son, I wish you good-night, and after sleep a happy madness.'

He turned with a smile to the Canon, who had come back with news of dinner, and was waiting impatiently behind us.

'I am not sleepy, I confess,' said the Canon, with a condescending laugh, 'and I still retain my sanity, but from your last words I conclude that you are confounding morality with works of supererogation, which the Church declares cannot be taught without arrogance and impiety.'

'I'm sure I never wished to dispute with churches or talk about morality,' said the shepherd sighing. 'I only know that in love and in war the works of supererogation are the things that count, and a good lover or a good fighter always does more than in bounden duty is required. That is the reason that I, a mere shepherd, have also become a curate to Venus and Mars. And so, when I die, please take my old parchment skin, shave it and dry it and stretch it tight to form the head of a hollow war-drum. But, for my heart, bray it in a mortar and pound it fine, that lovers may drink it as a charm.'

We had risen and were walking slowly towards the further gate of the Close. I wondered whether it would be in accordance with canonical law to ask a god to dinner, or whether it was not more usual to offer him a drink in the kitchen. Whilst I was hesitating to suggest either, for fear of what he might say to the servants, especially in consolation to poor Elizabeth, the Canon broke out rather irritably: 'I beg your pardon, my man, but I must really ask you again not to walk on the edge of our grass. You see it isn't common grass for sheep like the stuff you are accustomed to, and we are all very particular to keep it really nice. If I may say so, it is part of God's service, and I'm sure I don't know what the head-verger will say if he finds your footsteps on it in the morning!'

'He will think the beasts of the field have broken into the sanctuary, and that would be terrible!' cried the shepherd, and was gone.

I lit a match and examined the soft turf where he had been walking. It was all dinted with a cloven hoof. The Canon traced the marks with the point of his umbrella, and then looked up at me in wild surmise.

'The devil!' he exclaimed. And I do not know whether he was stating a scientific fact, or had forgotten himself for the first time in his life.

AN ENGLISHWOMAN'S LOVE-LETTERS

Small crown 8vo, 5s. net.

First Edition,	November 1900.
Second Impression,	December 1900.
Third Impression,	December 1900.
Fourth Impression,	December 1900.
Fifth Impression,	January 1901.
Sixth Impression,	January 1901.
Seventh Impression,	February 1901.
Eighth Impression,	March 1901.

PRESS OPINIONS.

'... charming letters, ... polished, but not too polished to be passionate, nor too passionate to overstep natural reticence.'—*The Spectator*.

Mr T. P. O'CONNOR in the *Daily Mail* says:—'I turned over the leaves rapidly, almost greedily, and had read almost all its story before I could allow myself to sleep. ... This little book, of which all London is now talking—of which London may still be talking many a generation hence. It is a loud cry, not merely of one intoxicated and torn heart, but of the claim of inner and true emotion to be still the greatest force of life; the one thing worth having—worth living for, longing for, dying for.'

'The true story of an actual life ... beautiful letters, beautifully written. ... Their author was a woman of great parts, of very refined sense ... It is much to say, but we remember nothing in literature quite so full of passionate human appeal as Letter LXXVII. ... Nothing could be more intensely human, no cry of human soul more passionate. Few will read it dry-eyed ... If there is any meaning in literature, if the most intimate of letters can express aught of human feeling, she was a woman to die for.'—*Vanity Fair*.

'We have not for a long time seen anything as pathetic as "An Englishwoman's Love-Letters" ... a tragedy and a record too sacred and too piteous for publication ... so great is their charm ... a tragedy, without plot, story, action, or incident ... it needs none of them ... this is not a book to quote or to review, but to read.'—*Literature*

'There will be many for whom these letters will have an extraordinary charm; many more cannot fail to respond to the intensity of the passion they reveal, and the depth of the tragedy they suggest, while the most critical and least emotional will find much to please them in the mere technical excellence of the writing. ... There are veins of deepest passion, of tender sentiment, delightful touches of humour, quaint revelations of a vanity, half childish, half womanly, which is exquisite by reason of its being inspired by love, glimpses without number into the soul of an adoring, adorable woman, and a note of tragic self-abnegation of a very rare kind ... to the most casual they must bring a heartache.'—*Daily Telegraph*.

LONDON: JOHN MURRAY, ALBEMARLE STREET, W.